HUMAN RIGHTS NOW!

HUMAN RIGHTS NOW!

THE OFFICIAL BOOK OF THE CONCERTS FOR HUMAN RIGHTS FOUNDATION WORLD TOUR

TEXT BY JAMES HENKE
INTRODUCTIONS BY PETER GABRIEL AND STING

FEATURING PHOTOGRAPHS BY ANNIE LEIBOVITZ,
NEAL PRESTON AND KEN REGAN

BLOOMSBURY

First published in Great Britain 1988

Bloomsbury Publishing Limited, 2 Soho Square, London W1V 5DE

ISBN 0-7475-0318-4

Photo credits:
All London-Barcelona concert photos: Ken Regan
All Costa Rica-Buenos Aires concert photos: Neal Preston
All other Neal Preston photos credited as marked
All Annie Leibovitz photos credited as marked

Photo Editor: Kim Ronis
Photo Assistant: Paul Schiraldi
Text Editor: Helen Armitage
Illustrations on pp. 12-20 by Robin Harris

Designed by Roy Williams and Laurence Bradbury
Design Assistants: Sarah Collins, Jenny May, Gill Sermon and Colin Woodman
Typeset by Bookworm Typesetting, Manchester and Denzil Graphics, London
Origination by Universal Colour Scanning Ltd, Hong Kong
Printed in Spain by Printer Industria Gráfica s.a., Barcelona

CONTENTS

FOREWORD BY JOHN G. HEALEY
6

INTRODUCTIONS BY PETER GABRIEL AND STING
8

'OH, BY THE WAY...':
THE ORIGINS OF THE HUMAN RIGHTS NOW! TOUR
10

THE PERFORMERS
22

THE BANDS
32

THE HUMAN-RIGHTS ACTIVISTS
33

THE CONCERTS
38

AMNESTY ADDRESSES AROUND THE WORLD
158

ACKNOWLEDGMENTS
160

FOREWORD BY JOHN G. HEALEY

HEAD OF CONCERTS FOR HUMAN RIGHTS FOUNDATION AND DIRECTOR OF AMNESTY INTERNATIONAL, USA

He moved around the world to get people around the world moving. The musicians started it, unleashing waves of energy on to their audiences. Audiences hurled waves of energy back on to the stage. Everybody—musicians and concertgoers—was awash with the kind of energy that causes change.

The Human Rights Now! musical tour started some changes that are going on right now. More people are hearing the cries of other people in need and casting out lifelines. More people are raising their voices with a clear, strong message for government throughout the world: we demand human rights now! The musicians sang out for rights, and the sound continues to reach further and further into people's hearts and minds.

Each concert—from Europe to Africa to Asia to the Americas—spread news of the basic rights belonging to every man, woman and child in the world. Musicians have these rights, music fans have them, you have them and I have them. It's news because so many people don't know about them or have only a vague idea of what they are. But when a government takes them away, the loss is devastating.

No government, at any time or in any place, should be allowed to deprive anyone of his or her basic human rights. Governments have said to themselves, and we've got it in writing. It's an amazing agreement and a precious possession of everyone. People have died in attempts to make this agreement a reality. People have been arrested for possessing a copy of it. The Human Rights Now! musical tour gave a copy of it to each concertgoer because this generation needs to know about its inheritance.

On 10 December this inheritance will be 40 years old. That's why the musicians and the Concerts for Human Rights Foundation chose this year for their musical tour. On 10 December 1948 the United Nations General Assembly proclaimed the Universal Declaration of Human Rights without dissent. The governments of the world agreed, for the first time in history, to a statement of every person's basic human rights. They pledged to recognize all people as free and equal in dignity and in their claim to basic rights. They promised to work towards a world without cruelty and injustice.

They didn't keep the promise. Everyone is supposed to be free from the cruelty of arbitrary arrest, unjust imprisonment and torture. But more than half of the world's governments gaol people in violation of their human rights. A third of the world's governments torture their prisoners.

Everyone is supposed to be free from the injustice of starvation and homelessness. But millions of people are starving, and countless are homeless.

Everyone has the right to be free from fear and free from want: that's what the Universal Declaration of Human Rights proclaims. We can hold governments to their promise if enough of us are committed to protecting human rights and to pouring enough energy into the commitment: that's what the Human Rights Now! musical tour proclaimed. The musicians and the music fans pledged to one another that they would try. They signed their copies of the Universal Declaration as a first step. Hundreds of thousands of signatures will be presented to the world's governments in December, signalling the potential of a new generation of human-rights activists.

The injustices and brutality in our world are legion, but it's our world and our responsibility to change it. The world-wide human-rights movement has made significant improvements in the past, and it can make more of them in the future. People unjustly imprisoned in some

countries have been freed, torture has been halted in some places, and many of the homeless and starving have been housed and fed. Now the momentum must increase. It all begins with individual people caring, then doing something to help individual people in need.

The musicians who performed at the Human Rights Now! concerts donated their talents and their time to changing things for the better, spreading the word about human rights. Dancers are dancing to spread the word, writers are writing and film-makers are making films. Teachers are teaching about human rights, and students are organizing for human rights. Everyone can help. Everyone can participate in the human-rights movement.

The Human Rights Now! tour urged people to do something practical right now: join Amnesty International. Amnesty volunteers come from over 130 countries. They're ordinary, decent, caring people who work to free prisoners of conscience — men, women and children who have been imprisoned solely because of their beliefs or ethnic origin and who have neither used nor advocated violence — to ensure fair trials for all political prisoners and to end torture and the death penalty. They regularly receive information about human rights, along with suggestions for action. Then they set to work.

Many Amnesty members write letters to government officials who are in a position to end human-rights abuses; some organize public events to raise awareness of human-rights issues; others brief journalists or hold vigils and petition-drives. All of them show the world's governments that individual people are watching what they do and are willing to mobilize whenever and wherever human-rights violations occur. They cause a groundswell of pressure. More and more govern-

ments, concerned about their international image, are responding to the pressure.

Amnesty International bases its work on the Universal Declaration of Human Rights. It is a non-partisan world-wide movement and a recipient of the Nobel Peace Prize. Amnesty's grass-roots membership is intent on creating an undeniable, irresistible force to protect human rights. Anyone who wants to help create this force can write to their local Amnesty organization for details of how to join.

The Human Rights Now! musical tour helped to renew the campaign for change. We want you to draw energy from the musicians and their music and from the thoughts and sounds that this book evokes in you. If you want to be part of the campaign, you can be. You have the capacity to care. Use it.

John G. Healey
Chairman of the Concerts for
Human Rights Foundation
and Executive Director
of Amnesty International USA

INTRODUCTIONS BY PETER GABRIEL AND STING

In 1986, I took part in the Conspiracy of Hope tour of the USA with U2, Sting, Lou Reed, the Neville Brothers, Bryan Adams and Joan Baez. It was great to see the impact we had. The membership of Amnesty International USA doubled, thousands of groups were formed in schools all over the country, and the cases of many prisoners of conscience were given a great deal of publicity. In all the press conferences, we outlined the cases of six prisoners of conscience, three of whom were successfully released. Most of all I learned from the many letters I received that those people who decided to get involved with Amnesty were excited to get a sense of their own power, realizing that they could change the fate of men and women many thousands of miles away from them.

The response to this tour encouraged some bold thinking, and I remember some early conversations about the possibility of taking the tour around the world. In March 1987, Jack Healey and Mary Daly outlined their vision of a world tour to Sting, Lou Reed and me at a dinner in New York City. It would focus on the Universal Declaration of Human Rights which was due to have its 40th anniversary in 1988. I read the Declaration later and was amazed to see the breadth of the articles. Not only did it cover protection of civil and political rights and freedoms, but it made clear that everyone was entitled to food, shelter, health care, education, employment, labour rights, maternity assistance and much more. All these rights existed regardless of race, sex, religion, political opinion or wealth.

Most people are unaware of their rights and the fact that their governments made a commitment to support and defend them 40 years ago. This information is powerful. The majority of the world's population is under 25. Music is their common language, perhaps the first universal language. We felt we could use our audience to get this information out.

As I write this, the tour is now in progress. It is a wonderful experience, the reactions inspiring. We are a group of artists with different styles and backgrounds, but there is a real sense of purpose and community. We have a lot of fun finding different ways of working together both in and out of music. I feel the press conferences are now much more effective and there's no doubt that the show has improved a great deal from its shaky start in London. All of the artists are people I would go out of my way to see. I am proud to be a part of this tour.

We are getting results. There are now hundreds of thousands of signatures in support of the Universal Declaration which will be delivered to the United Nations on 10 December. Those campaigning for human rights in each country seem to be getting a very positive charge from our presence and from the reactions of the audience.

As on the 1986 tour, we have travelling with us several human-rights activists, many have been the victims of human-rights abuses. I have found talking with them reminds me why we are here. When you listen first hand to the realities and horrors of their experience it is impossible not to be moved. It was on the Conspiracy of Hope tour that we first met one brave woman, Veronica, who had suffered terrible torture in the hands of the Chilean police. After the tour, her son Rodrigo returned to Chile to document what was hap-pening with his camera. He was stopped in the street by the military, covered with petrol and burned to death.

Also travelling with us is a South African civil-rights lawyer with many stories that I found very disturbing, including accounts of torture to children as young as seven and eight. However, I was happy to hear of her belief in the Universal Declaration of Human Rights. In many security trials, in which her defendants are not protected by South African law, she has only the Universal Declaration, which the South African government had agreed and approved, to refer to as a basic charter for justice.

The call for human rights must be turned from a cry into a roar. If enough voices from all around the world demand that their governments guarantee the rights defined in the Universal Declaration, we can give it the legal power to provide long-term protection for millions of people now oppressed and suffering.

In a world full of cynicism and pessimism, Amnesty International is a beacon of hope. It is the proof that ordinary people have power. Thousands of men and women have been rescued from unfair imprisonment, torture and execution by the simple act of letter writing. Now, more than ever, it is important for each one of us to recognize and use the power we have to bring about change. Even though governments have already promised these rights to their people, many have died in the struggle for them. We need a world which guarantees these rights for all its people. It is up to us to create it.

Peter Gabriel
São Paulo, Brazil
11 October 1988

My name is Sting. I'm a singer. I'm 36 years old, and I have four children. I've been a supporter of Amnesty International since 1981, when I learned about its work through participating in an entertainment called *The Secret Policeman's Ball*. I was part of the Conspiracy of Hope tour of 1986, along with Peter Gabriel and U2, among others. The tour was very successful on a number of levels, including money raised ($2.6 million) and new membership (over 100,000). It also generated a higher profile for Amnesty and vastly increased awareness about its activities and accomplishments. One of the high points of the tour was meeting and talking with the former prisoners who'd been freed, in part through the efforts of Amnesty.

This is an era when rock stars are constantly asked to lend their names to a multitude of worthy causes — some of which can be rather vague and woolly, along the lines of 'let's all hold hands and make the world a better place'. Somehow the logic of these events escapes me. When asked why I support Amnesty so strongly, I usually cite its focus on individuals. I want to tell you the story of one man to illustrate my point.

Sita Ram Maskey is a 39-year-old teacher of deaf children in the Kingdom of Nepal. As I write this, he is in prison. He has been neither charged nor tried. On 9 May 1987 he was picked up by the police in Kathmandu and sent to Bhadragol gaol on a detention order lasting nine months. Under the Public Security Act, this order can be repeated up to a maximum of three years for, among other things, breaching the 'peace and tranquillity inside the Kingdom of Nepal'. Sita Ram has served his first detention order. He is now on his second.

Conditions in Bhadragol gaol are terrible. The building itself is in a state of imminent collapse, and there is neither heating nor hot water. The prisoners, political and criminal alike, are kept 25 to a cell. Some are very violent. No food except for rice is provided, and there's not enough firewood to cook it on. All letters are censored. Sita Ram's wife has to travel 300 miles to visit him; she spends half her salary from the school for the deaf on fares. Sometimes she gets there, waits all day, and is not allowed to see her husband. She makes the journey home.

Sita Ram Maskey has no hope of even being considered for release until 1990. His crime? Organizing a protest against the sale of contaminated Polish milk powder manufactured at the time of the Chernobyl explosion. It seems to be in the nature of oppression that the very individuals who would effect positive change for the future are the people Amnesty has to protect.

Moving from the specific to the general in a variety of fields — environmental, political reform, work conditions and wages, housing and health, which affect all of us — once again, it is the focus on real people, with wives, children, addresses.

My hope is that this tour will have made Amnesty International more powerful in countries where human rights are not a given. I believe that Amnesty is one of the most civilized organizations in the history of the world. It effects justice through the writing of letters by ordinary people. I'm proud to have been on the Human Rights Now! tour, and I'm proud to have worked with Peter Gabriel, Bruce Springsteen, Youssou N'Dour and Tracy Chapman. We had a lot of fun, getting to know one another, tackling problems and singing together.

Sting
London, England
September 1988

'OH, BY THE WAY...': THE ORIGINS OF THE HUMAN RIGHTS NOW! TOUR

On 10 December 1948, the General Assembly of the United Nations adopted and proclaimed the Universal Declaration of Human Rights, the full text of which appears in the following pages. Following this historic act, the Assembly called upon all Member countries to publicize the text of the Declaration and 'to cause it to be disseminated, displayed, read and expounded principally in schools and other educational institutions, without distinction based on the political status of countries or territories'.

Javier Pérez de Cuéllar
**Javier Pérez de Cuéllar
SECRETARY-GENERAL**

All human beings are born with equal and inalienable rights and fundamental freedoms.

The United Nations is committed to upholding, promoting and protecting the human rights of every individual. This commitment stems from the United Nations Charter, which reaffirms the faith of the peoples of the world in fundamental human rights and in the dignity and worth of the human person.

In the Universal Declaration of Human Rights, the United Nations has stated in clear and simple terms the rights which belong equally to every person.

These rights belong to you.

They are your rights.

Familiarize yourself with them. Help to promote and defend them for yourself as well as for your fellow human beings.

The first time Jack Healey told American concert-promoter Bill Graham about his idea for a world-wide rock-and-roll tour on behalf of human rights, it sounded like an afterthought. Healey, the Executive Director of Amnesty International USA, and Graham were on the phone, taking care of some business left over from the Conspiracy of Hope, a six-city US tour sponsored by Amnesty in the summer of 1986. As the conversation began to wind down, Healey brought up one last subject.

'Oh, by the way, Bill,' Healey said, 'I have another idea . . .'

The idea Healey went on to describe was a vastly expanded version of the Conspiracy of Hope: a world-wide tour of rock-and-roll superstars that would simultaneously spread Amnesty International's message and celebrate the 40th anniversary of the signing of the Universal Declaration of Human Rights.

Graham, Healey says, loved the idea. 'I knew his mind saw the magic of it. He said he'd have to bring his son, David, along on the tour. And then he started laughing and said, "We'll have to call it the By the Way tour."'

Looking back, Graham remembers thinking it wasn't going to be easy. 'The countries Jack wanted to go to, Third World countries and so on, were uncharted territories for rock and roll, relative to the technical requirements of rock and roll and the logistics. And I knew that it would be extremely expensive. You'd have to find some way of covering the costs of doing shows where you can't charge what you charge in our country. And they needed a substantial line-up, commitments from major artists.'

In the months preceding that phone call, Jack Healey had been preoccupied with trying to figure out how to follow up the success of the Conspiracy of Hope. Though it lasted only two weeks, the

tour—which featured U2, Sting, Peter Gabriel, Bryan Adams, Lou Reed, Joan Baez, the Neville Brothers and others—had an enormous impact on Amnesty in the States, bringing in 100,000 new members and raising $2.6 million. Even more important, Healey remembers, 'We were able to get our message across, including the hardest part for Americans, which is to work against the death penalty.'

The tour had convinced Healey that rock and roll had a huge, and largely untapped, power—that it could convey Amnesty's message to what he considers the organization's most important constituency: young people. 'Half of the world's population is under 25, and almost half of the world can't read or write, so how are you going to reach those people and say, "Look, something's happening. A lot of people are getting killed, a lot of people are getting tortured"?'

How, Healey wondered, could he use the power of rock and roll to get that message across to the youth of the world?

While Healey was puzzling what to do, his associate, Mary Daly—another long-time Amnesty supporter and one of the executive producers of the Conspiracy tour—was mulling over the same question. 'We had seen this amazing success from the Conspiracy tour, but other Amnesty sections around the world were stagnating in a kind of bureaucratic quagmire,' Daly says. 'The European sections were decreasing in membership and weren't raising much money. The developing sections weren't developing. The whole movement seemed to be on the decline.'

One night in late October 1986, Daly was discussing this dilemma over dinner with David Hawk, a sixties anti-war activist and former head of Amnesty's US section. Hawk, who was still on the Amnesty board, was outraged by a proposal that would have channelled a significant portion of the profits from the Conspiracy tour into institutional development, such as a new computer system or an improved pension plan for Amnesty staff. He was adamant that the money should go towards *real* human-rights work, towards spreading Amnesty's message around the world. And he thought he knew just the right event around which Amnesty could build the sort of massive world-wide campaign he had in mind: the 40th anniversary of the signing of the Universal Declaration of Human Rights.

Drawn up after World War II and adopted by the United Nations on 10 December 1948, the Declaration outlines, in great detail, the civil, social, political and economic rights of every individual around the world. 'David said, "Why don't we tell the world its rights?"' Daly recalls. 'And I said, "How do we do that?" I immediately got real practical and started asking things like, "Do we do an ad campaign and take out ads all over the world? Or do we do a benefit? What?"'

The next morning, Daly called Healey. 'I told Jack about my conversation with David,' she says. 'He immediately got excited about the idea of doing something around the Declaration.'

That afternoon, Healey was having lunch with Martin Lewis, a film producer who had organized several previous Amnesty benefits. 'Jack had just gotten back from a vacation he'd taken to recuperate from the Conspiracy of Hope tour,' Lewis remembers, 'and, frankly, we both wanted to sit down and have a good gossip about the tour, a really good bitching session.'

But at one point, Healey mentioned Hawk's idea of focusing attention on the anniversary of the Universal Declaration. 'Jack was playing around with two concepts,' says Lewis. 'The first was a 24-hour rockathon, or some such thing, at Madison Square Garden. I thought it was a dreadful idea, and I told him so. I mean, who would want to spend 24 hours at Madison Square Garden?' The other idea was a world tour that would take place over the course of a couple of months and would include concerts in several countries around the world. Lewis found that far more appealing.

'We immediately started jotting down the names of countries we could play on the backs of our napkins,' Lewis says. 'We also figured out that the perfect timing would be the fall of 1988, right between the Olympics and the US presidential election. I thought they could make a splash in the media that way. They could really get people to pay attention to the message of the tour.'

Healey knew they'd latched on to something. 'If the human-rights movement can reach up and do something unusual once in a while to lower the pain level in the world, it has the responsibility to do that,' he says. 'And I felt we had some credibility with the music world and we ought to use it.'

John Cleese is probably the person Jack Healey should thank for that credibility. Though he wouldn't really qualify as a rock-and-roll fan, it was Cleese—the comedian and actor who's best known for his work with Monty Python's Flying Circus—who got Amnesty International started on the road that led to the Human Rights Now! tour.

By the mid-seventies Amnesty had begun to expand beyond its original base in England and Western Europe, but the initial excitement that had followed the group's founding in the sixties had started to wane. In addition, the organization was having trouble raising money. Cleese, a big Amnesty booster, decided to try and help and, in 1976, he volunteered to put together a benefit comedy show to celebrate Amnesty's 15th anniversary. Called *A Poke in the Eye (with a Sharp Stick)*, the show featured Monty Python and two other British comedy acts. The benefit was an instant hit, and after a subsequent TV special and record album, it raised around $40,000 for Amnesty.

Bolstered by his success, Cleese organized the *Mermaid Frolics* the next year. 'It followed the same formula as the first show,' says Martin Lewis, who co-produced the *Frolics* with Cleese. 'There was another album and another TV show, and we raised another $40,000.'

Lewis realized that if he and Cleese could

Article 1

All human beings are born free and equal in dignity and rights. They are endowed with reason and conscience and should act towards one another in a spirit of brotherhood.

Article 2

Everyone is entitled to all the rights and freedoms set forth in this Declaration, without distinction of any kind, such as race, colour, sex, language, religion, political or other opinion, national or social origin, property, birth or other status.

Furthermore, no distinction shall be made on the basis of the political, jurisdictional or international status of the country or territory to which a person belongs, whether it be independent, trust, non-selfgoverning or under any other limitation of sovereignty.

expand the appeal of their shows, they could raise even more money and make even more people aware of Amnesty. 'I thought that the thing to do was not to make a TV special, but to make a theatrically released film,' explains Lewis. 'And I thought, "wouldn't it be nice to add some pop music?"'

Lewis explained his idea to Cleese, who was game. He then approached Pete Townshend of the Who. Townshend was apprehensive, but ultimately agreed to appear as a solo act. *The Secret Policeman's Ball*, as the concert was called, took place in 1979—from 27 June to 30 June—and, in addition to several comedians, it featured another rocker, Tom Robinson, as well as the classical guitarist John Williams. This time, two records were released: a comedy album and a mini-album of music. The shows were also filmed, and a feature-length movie came out the following summer. In the end, *The Secret Policeman's Ball* raised more than $250,000.

The Secret Policeman's Other Ball—featuring Sting, Phil Collins, Donovan, Bob Geldof, Johnny Fingers, Eric Clapton and Jeff Beck—followed in September 1981, and in 1987 Amnesty put on yet another show, *The Secret Policeman's Third Ball*. But it was the first *Secret Policeman's Ball* that was the real breakthrough.

Two of the people who saw that show—and, as a result, heard about Amnesty for the first time—were Bono, the lead singer of U2, and Sting, at the time the lead singer and bass-player for the Police. In 1986, he and Bono became the first artists to volunteer when Jack Healey began putting together a US tour to celebrate Amnesty's 25th anniversary.

Once he'd decided to time the tour to coincide with the anniversary of the Universal Declaration of Human Rights, Healey set out to lay the groundwork. Meetings were held with influential music executives, several of whom embraced the idea.

But while those in the music business were offering their support, some of Healey's colleagues in Amnesty International weren't so keen on the idea—something both Martin

Lewis and Jamie Radner, the Director of Finance and Administration for Amnesty USA, found out when they mentioned the idea to some key Amnesty people in London.

'Jack had asked me to run the idea up the flag-pole when I got back to London,' Lewis remembers. 'And, to be honest, they were a little sceptical. To me, it was like a wonderful vision, and I couldn't see why they wouldn't be frothing at the mouth. But when I went back and told Jack their reaction, he wasn't surprised.'

'Our organization has never done central fund-raising before, or central anything, for that matter,' Healey explains. 'Nothing goes beyond an individual section's borders. You work in your section, you stay in your section. And so a new concept, working across Amnesty borders, which are national borders, involved a lot of talking, explaining, meeting. They were worried about funding it, about getting the musicians, about convincing governments to let us in. All of that.'

In part, that scepticism resulted from the fact that Amnesty International is perhaps the epitome of a decentralized organization. While the main headquarters in London serve as a sort of clearing-house for information about human-rights abuses throughout the world, almost everything else, including fund-raising, is left up to the national sections and their respective local groups. The members of those groups 'adopt' prisoners of conscience and work on their behalf by writing letters to government officials, seeking information about the prisoners, as well as their immediate and unconditional release. In other words, ordinary citizens around the world are working to help free other, less fortunate citizens.

The man who originated that concept, and founded Amnesty International, was a British lawyer and human-rights activist named Peter Benenson. In his book *Amnesty International: The Human Rights Story*, Jonathan Power describes the origin of Benenson's idea. 'In November 1960, his imagination was fired by a newspaper report about two Portuguese students in Lisbon during the dark days of the Salazár dictatorship. They had been arrested and sentenced to ten years' imprisonment for

Franca Sciuto, Chairperson, Amnesty International Executive Committee

raising their glasses in a public toast to freedom. How, Benenson wondered, could the Portuguese authorities be persuaded to release these victims of outrageous oppression? Somehow a way must be devised to bombard the Salazár regime with written protests.'

On Sunday 28 May 1961 an article written by Benenson entitled 'The Forgotten Prisoners' appeared in London's *Observer* newspaper, and it was subsequently syndicated in other papers around the world. In it Benenson launched his 'Appeal for Amnesty'. His goal, as Powers writes, was 'to work impartially for the release of those imprisoned for their opinions, to seek them a fair trial, to enlarge the right of asylum, to help political refugees find work, and to urge the creation of effective international machinery to guarantee freedom of opinion'.

Within a month, Benenson had received more than a thousand offers of help. By the end of 1961, Amnesty sections had been organized in seven countries and, within 12 months, Amnesty was actively investigating 210 cases. Today, Amnesty has more than 700,000 members in 150 countries, and the organization has sent over 500 missions to countries to carry out investigations, observe trials and meet with government officials.

But because so much of Amnesty's power lies with the individual sections, Healey's idea of a world-wide campaign was somewhat alien. However, he did have one important ally

among the Amnesty leaders: Franca Sciuto, an Italian lawyer and the Chairperson of Amnesty International's Executive Committee. 'My reaction was immediately very positive,' Sciuto says. 'It was more of a gut feeling; I just felt the time was right. I was immediately attracted to the idea of increasing human-rights awareness in our movement and, more important, around the world. We needed to build a new generation of people who were aware of what was happening in the world. And I felt that music, being a universal language, was the right tool to accomplish that.' Still, Sciuto realized that it might take some time to convince her colleagues.

Meanwhile, Healey was continuing to make progress back home in America. He set up a 'World Tour Team', which met at Amnesty's New York offices on 22 September 1987. The 11 people present—who included tour producers Mary Daly, Jamie Radner and Jessica Neuwirth, another key member of Amnesty's staff—drew up a list of goals for the tour. Half-way through that meeting, Healey and Daly left to meet with Bill Graham, who had agreed to help produce the tour. When they returned, they had bad news: Graham was having serious doubts about the feasibility of the project.

A veteran of almost 25 years in the music business, Graham is the dean of American concert-promoters and producers. In the sixties he ran the legendary Fillmore auditoriums in New York and San Francisco. Since then he has presented concerts by virtually every major rock act in the world and has produced world tours by such artists as the Rolling Stones and Bob Dylan. In addition, he has a long record of involvement in benefit and charity projects: the first show he ever staged was a benefit for the San Francisco Mime Troupe, and in 1985 he produced the American portion of Live Aid.

But Graham, strong-willed and opinionated, was concerned that Healey and the Amnesty people, with their almost naïve enthusiasm, weren't fully aware of just how huge a task they had undertaken—and he had no qualms about telling them what had been bothering him from the outset. A six-week world tour

Article 3

Everyone has the right to life, liberty and security of person.

Article 4

No one shall be held in slavery or servitude; slavery and slave trade shall be prohibited in all their forms.

Article 5

No one shall be subjected to torture or to cruel, inhuman or degrading treatment or punishment.

Article 6

Everyone has the right to recognition everywhere as a person before the law.

Article 7

All are equal before the law and are entitled without any discrimination to equal protection of the law. All are entitled to equal protection against any discrimination in violation of this Declaration and against any incitement to such discrimination.

Article 8

Everyone has the right to an effective remedy by the competent national tribunals for acts violating the fundamental rights granted him by the constitution or by law.

Article 9

No one shall be subjected to arbitrary arrest, detention or exile.

would be enormously expensive, he explained. The logistics would be a constant headache, and it would be difficult to get enough artists to make such a big commitment of time.

Still, his heart was with the project. He understood its importance. 'The issue is very clear to me: it symbolizes a man's right to freedom of expression. Freedom of stating your opinions. I believe in that, so if I'm asked to assist them, it just gets down to common sense, and common sense makes that decision.'

But to make such an ambitious tour a reality, it would take a lot more than common sense. As Graham puts it, 'Jack Healey is a constantly driven man, and without his mania, and the mania of a few other dedicated people, this tour wouldn't have happened.'

Almost from the start, it was determined that the Human Rights Now! tour would not be a Live Aid-style show with dozens of different acts jumping on stage for 15-minute sets of three or four of their greatest hits. 'Every night during the Conspiracy of Hope, I always wanted to hear more of each artist,' Healey recalls. 'I really thought, God, can't they stay out there longer? So we decided to choose a family—five or six artists who would really commit themselves and stay on the tour for six weeks. That way people would understand that this isn't a chic, fashionable thing, that they really are in there for a long period of time.'

Peter Gabriel was the first artist to make that commitment. 'I was very excited about the idea and offered my support straight away,' Gabriel confirms. 'From the point of view of a musician, the Conspiracy of Hope had been great fun. It really felt that there was a purpose much greater than just selling more records. It also tended to politicize me. The more you realize that you can have an effect, the harder it is to be lazy.'

Sting was the next to sign on. Like Gabriel, he had been inspired by the Conspiracy tour. 'The important thing was that we got new members,' he says. 'One hundred thousand new members, and they're still there, and they're still writing letters, and I think that's a

wonderful testimony to the success of that tour. So when asked if I would do it again, I said certainly, absolutely.'

The third artist who volunteered was the Senegalese singer Youssou N'Dour. A major pop star in Africa, N'Dour had been befriended by Gabriel, who had seen one of the singer's shows in Paris. Though he had long been aware of Amnesty, it was Gabriel's dedication to the organization that caused N'Dour to get involved. 'When I got to know Peter, we talked a lot about human commitment; when you're friends with someone, you have to talk about your personal feelings, your commitments. And Peter was very committed to Amnesty, so we spent a long time talking about it. And I decided that I, too, should be involved with Amnesty and put as much time into it as I could.'

With Sting, Gabriel and N'Dour, Healey felt he had the core of talent needed to carry out the tour. Meanwhile, other artists began to offer their services. Robbie Robertson volunteered to do the entire tour. Eric Clapton said he'd do part of it. George Michael offered to play at least one date. 10,000 Maniacs wanted to be involved. Suzanne Vega and Robert Cray said they were interested. So did INXS and Paul Simon. There was also talk of a Who reunion, or a Cream reunion.

But Graham still wasn't convinced that they had a solid enough bill to ensure the tour's success. As Peter Gabriel remembers, 'I spoke to Bill, and he told me, "Listen, we've got a lot of vegetables, but we need a steak."'

At first sight, Jack Healey appears about as unlikely a candidate to organize a rock-and-roll tour as one could imagine. Balding and bespectacled, he looks more like an absent-minded professor than a visionary. His glasses are crooked, his tie rumpled; his clothes look slept in. When he talks he seems distracted and has a tendency to mumble and fidget. But get him on a subject that really matters to him—a subject like human rights—and another Jack Healey emerges. This Jack Healey is confident, convincing and passionate, a gifted speaker whose voice, punctuated with the pain and suffering of the world's needy, possesses that rare ability to move people.

Healey was born 50 years ago in a lower middle-class Irish Catholic family in Pittsburgh, Pennsylvania. His father died in a car accident when Jack was only two. His mother, who was left with 11 children and virtually no money, 'believed in people with a passion', Healey says. 'She believed in fighting the rich and doing battle. You were not to come into this world and leave easily.'

As a kid, Healey did battle—though not the kind his mother had in mind. 'I did crazy things: drinking, carrying on, stealing cars, fighting. I thought it was fun. Shut the school down, lock the teachers out, anything. Breaking into theatres.'

Fortunately, as Healey's antics were beginning to take a more dangerous turn, a Catholic priest intervened. 'He said, "You're too smart for this. You ought to do something with your life." And he asked if I wanted to enter the seminary.' Healey, who was 18 at the time, agreed to give it a try for the summer. 'I didn't like it at all,' he remembers. 'But the priest talked me into going back, trying it again. I did, and I liked it.'

Healey went on to graduate in philosophy from St Fidelia College and in theology from Capuchin College. In 1964 he joined the Franciscan fathers. Soon after, his mother's influence began to show as he became caught up in the civil rights and anti-war movements that were spreading through the US. Healey took part in protest marches and other activities—such as supporting a strike by janitorial workers against a Catholic hospital—deemed 'unpriestly' by some of his superiors. At one point he was assigned to teach a catechism class. 'I told the kids that North Vietnamese children were as good as South Vietnamese children,' Healey says. 'The kids went home and told their parents—and I never taught again.'

Around Christmas 1968 Healey decided to leave the priesthood. 'I was just bored. I couldn't find enough work. And I didn't know how to make it work. I didn't like the Church's ceremonies for baptism and marriage. I didn't teach catechism. So it was like I had to make my job up every day. And I didn't want that.'

But without the Church to support him,

Healey was a little lost. 'I was 30 years old, I was still a virgin. And I didn't have any money.' Still, he survived, eventually becoming Deputy Director of the American Freedom from Hunger Foundation. In this capacity he devised the first ever walkathon, teamed up with comedian-turned-activist Dick Gregory for the 1976 World Hunger Run from Los Angeles to New York, and ultimately raised $10 million to aid the world's starving.

In 1977 President Jimmy Carter appointed Healey head of the Peace Corps in the small African country of Lesotho. It was while serving there that Healey heard that Amnesty's US section was looking for a new Director. He applied, and in 1981 was named the section's Executive Director.

During his six years in that position, Healey has turned Amnesty—once virtually unknown in the US—into a household name, raising millions of dollars and gaining thousands of new members in the process. Healey is a master organizer with a keen ability to capture the public's attention. He's also a shrewd operator who knows how to manœuvre his way through potentially explosive situations and who has made himself right at home in the world of rock and roll. As one of his co-workers put it, 'He's like a cross between Bill Graham and Henry Kissinger.'

On 9 December 1987—the eve of International Human Rights Day—the leaders of Amnesty International gathered in São Paulo, Brazil, for a press conference to announce the organization's five-point plan to publicize the anniversary of the Universal Declaration. And so, in her opening remarks, Franca Sciuto, the Amnesty Chairperson, told the press about 'a series of popular concerts in support of the campaign for human rights. We hope to see live performances in 15 to 20 countries. The aim will be to go world-wide and reach audiences in as many regions as possible.'

Sting, who was on tour in South America, appeared at the press conference, as did Gabriel, N'Dour, Graham and such prominent South American artists as Milton Nascimento and Gilberto Gil. But despite the outward

John G. Healey, Executive Producer of the Human Rights Now! Tour and Executive Director, Amnesty International USA section

display of unity, Healey and Mary Daly were having to work overtime to convince the Amnesty leadership that they were doing the right thing. At one late-night meeting before the press conference, they again attempted to explain the project. 'Everybody came, and the energy level was really high,' Healey recalls. 'A lot of them had problems with the tour, but when all was said and done, an awful lot of them wanted us to come and play. Just automatically—come and play.'

Still, there were several unresolved issues. 'Many of the people in the Amnesty leadership still wanted this to be a fund-raising event for the European sections. They couldn't understand that we were talking about an *awareness* event,' Daly says. 'And they had other problems. They didn't want it to go to the Soviet Union, for example. And they were afraid of having the artists speaking to the press on Amnesty's behalf.'

A couple of days before the press conference, Gabriel went to dinner with Sciuto and Ian Martin, the Secretary General of Amnesty. 'Peter really laid out a whole set of strategies and possibilities for the tour,' Daly says. 'And later, he and Sting talked to Franca and Ian for a long time about how important it was to do the Third World and the Eastern Bloc. And I think that Franca and Ian really got sold on the artists as serious human-rights activists. In a lot of ways, the artists were clearer and more measured about how this could happen than

Jack and I had been in the whole year of meetings we had with Amnesty.'

Jack Healey looks back on the period before and after that press conference as the lowest point of the almost two years of planning that went into the tour. 'Those were the darkest days,' he says. 'I didn't see my way out. I really didn't.'

The problem was money. Early on, Healey had got the US section of Amnesty to donate $250,000 to the project. As those funds began to dwindle, he secured other contributions: $25,000 from the Canadian section of Amnesty, and donations from several record-company and music-business executives. But now, more than a year after Healey had first started discussing the tour, the money was running out.

To complicate matters further, the estimated cost of the tour was skyrocketing. The initial estimate had been around $15 million. But as the tour's organizers began looking into the actual expense of taking five or six bands around the world, the estimate ballooned to $22 million.

Healey and Jamie Radner, the tour's financial officer, were forced to come to terms with the fact that it would be virtually impossible to raise that much money solely through the usual sources of tour revenue, such as the sales of tickets and souvenir merchandise. Those sources, they figured, would bring in about $9 million, while another $3 million or so might be raised by selling broadcasting rights to some of the shows. But that still left a deficit of about $10 million, and the only way they could cover that deficit would be if someone—most likely a corporation—was willing to make a substantial donation. And for Healey, that was not a welcome realization.

'It was very hard for me to come to terms with that,' he says. 'I've never worked for a corporation. I've never wanted to. I'm deeply suspicious of them.'

Initially, Healey envisioned a coalition of five or six corporations that would contribute about a million dollars each. 'We never thought that in the capitalistic system of the United States we would be able to find one corporation that would be smart enough to underwrite the whole thing, and yet do it in a minimal way.'

But in fact, such a company did exist. Reebok, the manufacturer of athletic shoes, had seen its US sales grow from $1.3 million in 1981 to nearly $1.4 *billion* in 1987, and the company was searching for a way to cement its reputation among young people. 'We were looking around for something that would allow us to stand for something,' explains Angel Martinez, Reebok's vice-president for business development. 'We had grown so fast in the last eight years that there had been no time to say, "What do we want to be when we grow up?" And it became obvious that the issue of human rights was something that was moving young people.'

That issue also had a certain amount of personal relevance to Martinez, who left his native country of Cuba when he was three and who hasn't been able to see his parents or his two sisters since he last visited them there in 1960. 'Nobody realized when the gate went down in 1961 that it would still be down in 1988,' he says.

Reebok's advertising agency, Chiat/Day, made the first approach to Amnesty, and an initial meeting was set up with Reebok's executives. 'This ill-dressed little fellow, Jack Healey, who was very underwhelming, walked in and began to talk about what they were trying to accomplish,' remembers Reebok's president and chief operating officer, C. Joseph LaBonté. 'And I've got to tell you, he is a marvellous person. He was captivating, he was committed, he believed. And he wasn't giving us a pitch. He was taking about what he does, and what his life is about. And he was so passionate about what they were trying to accomplish and why music really made a difference. And at the end of that, I was really taken aback with what Amnesty stood for, and how it dovetailed, in an interesting way, with what we stood for.'

In a matter of days, LaBonté returned with a proposal that floored the tour organizers: Reebok didn't just want to make a contribution, the company wanted to underwrite the entire tour.

'In about a week, we had an agreement,' Healey recalls. 'Reebok would underwrite the deficit up to $8 million, and they would front us another $2 million so we could keep the thing going.' In addition, the company instituted the Reebok Foundation Human Rights Award, an annual award of $100,000 that would be shared by two human-rights activists, one male and one female, under the age of 30.

Healey, the artists and Amnesty all had their own concerns about establishing such close ties with a corporation. Because of his strong anti-corporate sentiment, Healey was asked by Amnesty to oversee the negotiations. To start with, he had several public-interest groups look into Reebok's background to make sure the company had no ties that could embarrass Amnesty, particularly in the Third World. He was pleased with what he found. 'Reebok had just renewed its contracts in Taiwan and South Korea, and those contracts seemed to be honourable in the context of those countries,' says Healey. 'And they have no holdings in South Africa, so they came up clean on that side, too.'

Though the relationship was hardly problem-free, Healey, at least, emerged relatively content. 'This has been a very graceful relationship between them as a corporation and our organization, which is massively dedicated to its independence and integrity. We won't allow anybody to play with that. They haven't, and that's very honourable.'

With the money now in hand, the nightmarish task of developing a workable itinerary had to be dealt with. Much of the responsibility for co-ordinating the logistical aspects of that project had been given to Michael Ahern, another music-business veteran, whose professional history stretches from the early seventies, when he was stage manager at Graham's Fillmore East, to 1987, when he directed David Bowie's Glass Spider tour.

Ahern had also been tour director for the Conspiracy of Hope, so it was only natural that he should be enlisted for this project. He agreed to take on the task and various

Article 22

Everyone, as a member of society, has the right to social security and is entitled to realization, through national effort and international co-operation and in accordance with the organization and resources of each State, of the economic, social and cultural rights indispensable for his dignity and the free development of his personality.

Article 23

1 Everyone has the right to work, to free choice of employment, to just and favourable conditions of work and to protection against unemployment.

2 Everyone, without any discrimination, has the right to equal pay for equal work.

3 Everyone who works has the right to just and favourable remuneration ensuring for himself and his family an existence worthy of human dignity, and supplemented, if necessary, by other means of social protection.

4 Everyone has the right to form and to join trade unions for the protection of his interests.

Article 24

Everyone has the right to rest and leisure, including reasonable limitation of working hours and periodic holidays with pay.

itineraries were drawn up. One early schedule included dates in Australia and New Zealand, but those countries were dropped because of the excessive amount of time and money it would take to get there. Gabriel made a strong pitch for Nicaragua, which he had visited in 1987, but he was eventually overruled. Not only did the country lack the necessary facilities, but also there were obvious political considerations: rather than choose between the leftist Sandinista government in Nicaragua and the right-wing leadership in El Salvador, it was decided that it might make a stronger statement if the tour stopped in Costa Rica, as a show of support for President Oscar Arias's Central American peace plan. Another early itinerary also included Youssou N'Dour's native country, Senegal, but a curfew was imposed in the wake of the presidential elections there, and it was decided to play Côte d'Ivoire instead. The Philippines was also considered, but the potential for violence was deemed too great.

Some of the most difficult negotiations, however, were those involving countries in the Eastern Bloc and the Third World. In Eastern Europe, Amnesty made official enquiries in Poland, Hungary and Yugoslavia. Poland and Hungary refused. Yugoslavia said yes, and plans got under way for a show in Ljubljana. But a site inspection by Ahern and his team found that the best venue in Ljubljana was 'a local football pitch' that hardly met the tour's logistical requirements. Fortunately, at about the same time, a change in government in Hungary prompted Amnesty to reapply, and in early July permission was granted for a show in Budapest.

There were also prolonged negotiations with the Soviet Union. The tour organizers—particularly Gabriel—felt it was crucial that the USSR be on the itinerary. Amnesty's leadership, on the other hand, was dead set against it. For years, the Soviet Union had refused to recognize Amnesty; no amnesty missions were allowed into the country, and the Government would not co-operate with any Amnesty investigations. However, with the advent of *glasnost* came a chance to restore ties, and Amnesty's leaders felt that the tour might

in some way jeopardize their negotiations with the Russians. 'They were telling us that we didn't really understand the complexities of Amnesty's relationship with the Soviet Union,' Mary Daly recalls. 'And that may have been true. But we felt there were ways we could make it happen that would be beneficial to both Amnesty and the Soviets.'

Gabriel's meeting with Ian Martin and Franca Sciuto around the time of the press conference in Brazil helped lessen Amnesty's concern. Then, around the middle of 1988, Martin began holding meetings with the Russians in an effort to get them to allow an Amnesty mission into the country. At one point during those negotiations Martin happened to mention the tour, and the Soviet representative responded favourably, opening the door for further talks.

Shortly after that, Bill Graham began talks with the Soviet Peace Commission, the group that had helped him arrange a 4 July concert by several American artists in Moscow in 1987. Meanwhile, several informal approaches were also made, making use of contacts that various artists, novelists, politicians and newsmen had in the Soviet Union. Negotiations continued throughout the tour, and the question of whether the Russians would permit a concert in Moscow became a major issue on the road.

One of the tour's other shows—in Mendoza, Argentina, on the border of Chile—came about in yet another way. Notorious for the human-rights violations that have taken place under General Augusto Pinochet's regime, Chile has been heavily criticized by Amnesty, and the tour organizers knew there was little chance of the country's permitting a show within its borders. But Ariel Dorfman, an exiled Chilean poet who teaches at the University of North Carolina, phoned Healey with the idea of having a concert on the border, telling him of a mountain pass by which Chileans could make their way to the stadium in Mendoza. 'He said he had been told that I was the only person crazy enough to go along with this idea,' Healey says. 'And he was right—I loved it!'

In the end, the tour managed to reach just

On 3 July, 1988, the official announcement of the Human Rights Now! Tour is made to reporters at London's Amnesty International headquarters.

about every corner of the world, with the exception of Australasia—an amazing feat, given not only the technical and logistical requirements, but also the politically controversial message it was conveying.

In early May, Peter Gabriel flew to San Francisco, intent on meeting Bruce Springsteen and persuading him to take part in the tour. Typically reticent, Gabriel, who showed up unannounced at one of Springsteen's shows near San Francisco, never got to talk to Bruce. But he did manage to get a ride back to the city on the band's bus. Heavy traffic delayed the trip for almost an hour, and Gabriel found he had plenty of time to make his pitch to Jon Landau, Springsteen's manager.

'I really bent his ear,' Gabriel says. 'I told him how important I thought the tour was, and how I thought the Universal Declaration of Human Rights was potentially a really powerful instrument of change.'

A couple of weeks later, back in New York, Healey got a call from Frank Barsalona, the head of Premier Talent, the agency that books Springsteen's shows. 'Frank said, "Tell me about your tour,"' Healey remembers. 'Then he asked if I would like to meet Jon Landau.' A meeting was set up for the afternoon of 19 May, and Healey, Landau and Barsalona spent four or five hours going over almost every aspect of the tour. At the end of it, Landau invited Healey to Springsteen's show that night at Madison Square Garden.

'I went backstage after the show, and Bruce was sitting in this little empty room, wearing this white terry-cloth robe. He had lots of

questions—intelligent ones. He asked me to tell him about the human-rights movement. About what Amnesty did in the US. Did we represent the American Indians? What do we do about the death penalty? Things like that.

'He also said that if he did a tour like this one, he really wanted to see the countries, to know where he was and to meet the activists. And he wanted to meet victims of torture.'

After about 30 minutes, Springsteen asked Healey how he could help. 'I told him I'd like him to do the whole tour, the whole damn thing. And he said, "Okay, let's do it!"'

On 3 July 1988, Franca Sciuto once again faced the press. 'Forty years ago, the governments of the United Nations made a historic promise to the world,' she said. 'They proclaimed, for the first time in history, that all human beings would be recognized as free and equal in dignity and rights. This was the promise of the Universal Declaration of Human Rights... That promise has not been kept.'

Sciuto, Healey, Graham and Harvey Goldsmith, a London-based concert-promoter who had been crucial in helping to organize many of the shows, went on to announce officially that Bruce Springsteen and the E Street Band, Sting, Peter Gabriel, Youssou N'Dour and Tracy Chapman, an American singer-songwriter, would embark on the Human Rights Now! tour, beginning on 2 September at Wembley Stadium in London. 'With music, we can communicate to all people equally well in the rich and poor nations of the East and West,' Healey told the reporters who'd assembled at Amnesty's London headquarters. 'And

Article 27

1 Everyone has the right freely to participate in the cultural life of the community, to enjoy the arts and to share in scientific advancement and its benefits.

2 Everyone has the right to the protection of the moral and material interests resulting from any scientific, literary or artistic production of which he is the author.

Article 28

Everyone is entitled to a social and international order in which the rights and freedoms set forth in this Declaration can be fully realized.

we can demand that governments give human rights now.'

A few hours later, in a stadium near Stockholm in Sweden, Bruce Springsteen approached the microphone. 'Earlier today, Amnesty International announced a world-wide tour to celebrate the 40th anniversary of the Universal Declaration of Human Rights,' Springsteen told the crowd—as well as hundreds of thousands of other people who were listening to the show via a live radio broadcast. 'The Declaration of Human Rights is a document that was signed by every government in the world 40 years ago, recognizing the existence of certain inalienable human rights for everyone, regardless of your race, your colour, your sex, your religion, your political opinion or the type of government that you're living under.

'I was glad to be asked to participate and I'm proud to join Sting, Peter Gabriel, Youssou N'Dour and Tracy Chapman in a tour that's gonna begin in early September and that's gonna run about six weeks. So I'd like to dedicate this next song to the people at Amnesty International and their idea. And when we come to your town, come on out, support the tour and support human rights for everyone now and let freedom ring.' Springsteen then went into 'Chimes of Freedom', a song that Bob Dylan had recorded and written back in 1964 and that would become the unofficial theme of the Human Rights Now! tour.

The pregnancy for dreams is always difficult,' says Peter Gabriel, 'and the bigger the dream, the more difficult the pregnancy.' On more than one occasion Jack Healey thought he should step down. So did Bill Graham. And Mary Daly. Even Peter Gabriel—the tour's strongest pillar of emotional strength—had his moments of doubt. But, throughout all the trials and tribulations, there was an underlying knowledge that everyone was working to bring about something that was far more important than just another rock-and-roll tour. One moment stands out for the Amnesty organizers, a moment when they were forcefully confronted with the import-

ance of their on-going commitment and encouraged to continue, despite all the doubt and frustration. In March 1988 about 70 people gathered at a Los Angeles restaurant to celebrate Jack Healey's 50th birthday. The restaurant was full of Healey's friends and acquaintances from various walks of life—people from the human-rights movement, from rock and roll, from politics, from Hollywood. Daryl Hannah was there. So was Jackson Browne. So were Sting and his manager, Miles Copeland. And so was Reebok's Angel Martinez. Near the end of the evening, one of the guests, Bishop Simon Farisani, a former South African prisoner of conscience, stood up to speak.

'I used to talk to Amnesty International groups, and I used to say, "Thank you for what you've done,"' the Bishop said in his booming voice. 'But now I talk to them and I say, "Why don't you do more?"'

Farisani went on to talk about the real importance of a project like the Human Rights Now! tour—about how even though any human being can take another human being and, with the authority of government, can beat them, humiliate them, put them in prison and kill them, there is still some spirit in individuals that resists that, and there are still people around the world who will tell governments to stop. And all that is valid and important, Farisani said, but it's still not enough.

'There was something in the way he said that,' Mary Daly recalls, 'that rejuvenated everyone. Sting was rejuvenated. Angel Martinez and the people from Reebok knew why they were in this. Everyone suddenly remembered why we were doing this tour. And things like that just had a way of occurring all along the way.'

And in many ways, that's the real story of the Human Rights Now! tour: how everyone involved—the promoters, the artists, the organizers, the media people and so on—managed to work together and support one another in the face of almost impossible odds. And they did it for one reason: so that their dream—human rights *now*—could become everyone's dream.

THE PERFORMERS

THE BANDS

THE HUMAN-RIGHTS
ACTIVISTS

B ecause of Amnesty International, the world's politicians have to be more careful. In its own way, Amnesty is more powerful than these politicians, and I think it is good to put the politicians — who, for me, are the real villains — in their place, to show them with music and musicians.

'In Africa, there are many problems; there are many problems in the Third World. And those problems are obvious. Everyone knows that, say, the president has 17 people in prison. In the developed countries, like America, politicians can hide the problems so that you can't see them.

'But music is the one aspect of the culture that can really and truly pass a message on. The most popular songs in Africa are the ones with a message, and the message may be a little harsh, but the people need that. They need to know the truth. They need to know the truth, because there's not much truth going around in Africa.

'I think that this tour turned loose something that's very pure, something that's never happened before. I think that we'll see that it really shook up the way people see things, and that its effect will last for a long time.'

think that Amnesty International, as an organization, does good work, and one of the reasons I got involved in this tour is because I think it's important that people be made aware of what Amnesty does, the kinds of concerns that the organization has, and the kinds of things it is accomplishing by making human-rights violations known to people throughout the world.

'As a black American, and an American in general, I have a real interest in the quality of people's lives in the United States, and that's reflected in my music. As a country, we tend to look outside instead of looking inside when it comes to human rights; people don't see the United States in the same way that they see other countries. But we clearly violate people's human rights in the States. And maybe this tour will have caused some people, particularly in America, to re-examine their own lives and to see in what ways people are suffering and in what ways they may be able to help.

'I also hope this tour will have encouraged people from all over to get involved. I hope it will have raised people's consciousness around the world, and maybe it will have put some pressure on governments to make changes for the people.

'The really wonderful thing about this tour is that as far as communicating to people is concerned, music is universal. Even if you don't understand the words to a song, you can feel the rhythm of it. You can appreciate the melody. And from those things you can get a sense of the emotions behind a song.

'This tour was the chance of a lifetime — to have performed in the places we performed in and, on top of that, to have it all mean something, too.'

PETER GABRIEL

*B*efore we started planning this tour, the Universal Declaration of Human Rights was something I had heard of but had never read. And until I read it, I had no idea how far-reaching it is. When you get into it, you find out that it deals with things like the socio-economic aspects of human rights: the right to have a decent standard of living, adequate health and well-being; the right to have things like food, clothing, housing, medical care and a free education.

'I genuinely believe that this document is potentially a very powerful instrument of change. One of the goals of the tour was to publicize the fact that the Declaration has been approved by many of the world's governments. I'm not sure how many of those governments are fully aware of its content. And obviously the only way the articles in the Declaration can become law, the only way they can be brought into the legal framework of countries throughout the world, is by generating enough popular support for the document.

'I also hope this tour encouraged people to get involved in the process of change, that it made them feel more powerful and gave them another way of looking at human rights; and that it clearly demonstrated the principle that anyone, anywhere, regardless of race, colour, creed or sex, should enjoy the rights specified in the Declaration.

'Idealism tends to be eroded by fear. But it can be re-established or built up through unity. And I hope that's what this tour demonstrated — unity among all those people around the world who are working to achieve and guarantee human rights.'

very day I'm asked to lend my name to different causes, from children's homes to cancer research, from people trying to stop the seal kills to people trying to protect the rain forests. But human rights is the umbrella that protects all the other issues, because very often the people who are going to effect change are the people who are in prison. And the fact that Amnesty International focuses on individuals — real people with real names in real photographs — appeals to me more than just throwing money at a problem in a willy-nilly way.

'Amnesty's currency is the written word. Its weapon is the letter. I believe in Amnesty's non-violence, I believe in its effectiveness, its dignity and its sense of commitment. And it makes me feel more human to be associated with Amnesty.

'We who live in Western Europe and North America have a fair belief that if we're arrested, we won't be tortured, we won't be imprisoned without a trial, we won't be murdered. Generally, human rights are a given. But that is not the case in the developing world. The people there live in a medieval atmosphere — the police do torture you; you can be shot in the street. And, in a sense, the idea of this tour was to take Amnesty's message closer to that theatre.

'It's all very nice singing about freedom in Milwaukee, but people in Milwaukee are free. It's quite another thing to go somewhere like South America. When you sit and talk to a prisoner of conscience — someone who has been tortured, arrested in the night, beaten up, imprisoned — the drama in your own life is suddenly diminished.'

When I was a kid, I went downtown and bought a single. I think it was "Like a Rolling Stone". And everybody, including my mother and father, thought it was just a little piece of plastic, a piece of junk. But when I put the single on the record-player, I found a transcendent moment of freedom that touched and changed my life. And that sense of freedom was very raw and non-political. It struck straight at my heart and my guts. And I think that's what rock at its best makes — it makes freedom. And, as far as I can see, that's what Amnesty International does, too. At the moment, I don't think there's a more important organization in the world than Amnesty International, and that's why I did this tour. I think that Amnesty makes the world a less oppressive, less brutal place to live in, and I wanted to help Amnesty do its job.

'When you're young and you pick up a guitar, it feels so powerful. It feels like you pulled the sword from the stone. But as you get older, you realize that, although it can do a lot of things, there are also a lot of things it can't do. I used to believe that it could save the world, but I don't really believe that any more. I do believe that it can save a life, or it can save time in someone's life. When somebody comes to one of our shows, they hear what we're singing about and they hear about Amnesty International. And if that person goes home and writes a letter, and someone ends up getting out of prison early — well, that's pretty good.

'As I've got older, one of the things I've wanted to do with my music is somehow to take that power that I got from those records when I was a kid and put it to work in some nuts-and-bolts way. And I've tried to find out who the people are out there who are working in the trenches, who are taking those ideas and ideals — same ideas and ideals that I got from those records — and putting them to use in some pragmatic way. The people who, inch by inch, or letter by letter, are making the world a little less hateful, a little more open, a little freer. Who's doing that? Well, Amnesty International is doing exactly that, so when this tour came up, I said if they need my help, that's where I want to put my energy.'

THE BANDS

Youssou N'Dour's band:
From left to right:
Bottom: Habib Faye, Papa Oumar Ngom
Middle: Babacar Faye, Youssou N'Dour, Marietou Kote
Top: Abdoulaye Mane, Assane Thiam, Mamadou Dieng

Gabriel's band:
From left to right:
Shankar, David Rhodes, Peter Gabriel, David Sancious, Darryl Jones, Manu Katche

Springsteens band:
Left to right:
Bottom: Roy Bittan, Nils Lofgren
Middle: Patti Scialfa, Bruce Springsteen, Danny Federici
Top: Clarence Clemons, Max Weinberg, Garry Talent

Sting's band:
From left to right:
Bottom: Sting, Mino Cinelu
Middle: Dolette McDonald, Tracy Wormworth, Jeff Campbell
Top: Delmar Brown, Branford Marsalis, Kenny Kirkland, J.T. Lewis

As one of the human-rights activists, Scharlette Holdman, put it, 'Our purpose on this tour is to be a link between the artists and people like us who live the daily struggle for justice. We try to remind them that human rights is not just a principle.'

SCHARLETTE HOLDMAN

Scharlette Holdman is one of the United States' most important anti death-penalty activists. Born into a white, wealthy southern family, she became active in the civil-rights movement during the sixties. By the mid-seventies, her attention shifted to the rights of prisoners on death row. She is currently the director of the Florida division of the Southern Coalition for Jails and Prisons. Florida has 600 people on death row — the largest number in the country. Although the common image of a death-row prisoner may be of a crazed, remorseless serial killer, according to Holdman, these prisoners are more likely to be minorities, many with mental disabilities and/or very low IQs, still others are Vietnam Veterans suffering from Post Traumatic Stress Disorder. Holdman tells numerous stories about men she's tried to save: 'Electrocution is torture. After someone's executed you can see the burnt raw flesh where the electrodes were attached, the curled fingers and the swollen body. Some men don't mind being cremated because they know their body will have been so disfigured. But one man, David Funchess, was religiously opposed to cremation. David was a young, black man who'd won five medals as a marine in Vietnam and he came back to Jacksonville, Florida horribly destroyed by the war. He had Post Traumatic Stress Disorder. He'd stepped on a land-mine and been terribly injured. They put him on morphine which led to his heroin addiction. David dug a foxhole under his mother's home and lived in it. He did about five bags of heroin a day and he would beg for that, but one day he robbed a liquor store and killed three people. And he lived with that remorse and pain for the remaining years of his life until he was executed. We claimed the body in a wooden coffin and drove him to my house. I sat up with him that night. I was in my carport with his body and I thought he deserved a wake, and I don't believe in God but I used my beliefs and stayed with him. The next day we buried him in a pasture on his volunteer attorney's farm. David's only request was that we play the Marine Anthem. . . . You think about the children and what we tell them — that we're killing their fathers. We see children stand in the prison hallways and beg and cry "please don't kill my daddy" as these men are led down the corridors to be executed. What can you say to that child? The last night before an execution, children want to be with their fathers, mothers with their sons, sisters with their brothers and, for all the world in me, I always want them not to want to be there, but they always want to . . . as you would.'

ARN CHORN

Arn Chorn was nine years old when the Khmer Rouge took over Cambodia. Like millions of other Cambodians, Chorn was separated from his family (he has not seen them since) and forced to live in a Khmer Rouge camp. He and about 500 other children in this particular camp were made to work all day. If they cried, they were killed. When the Vietnamese invaded Cambodia in 1978, the Khmer Rouge forced Chorn and the other children to fight. After the Khmer Rouge was pushed into the jungle by

Arn Chorn

the Vietnamese, Chorn was separated from the other children. He spent two months alone in the jungle, surviving by following troops of monkeys and eating the food they let fall from trees. Eventually, he crossed into Thailand only to be placed in a Khmer Rouge camp by the Thais. Chorn lived there for two years and once again saw people dying around him every day. He was fourteen years old and weighed fifty pounds. In 1980 he was adopted by Reverend Pond, an American living in New Hampshire. Chorn-Pond now attends Brown University and is a co-founder of Children of War, a peace organization that sends children who have experienced war to speak at schools about the horrors they've witnessed and to urge other children to work for peace: 'I was forced to live with 500 kids. There was killing every day, sometimes three times a day. Most of the time the kids were forced to watch. Most mornings we got up at five or six and many times we were not given food. And nobody dared to ask why. For me killing is my daily life. One time I came out of the temple, trying to find some food on the ground. And the Khmer Rouge took seven people, one woman and six men, all naked, and tied them up. There's no trial at all. One Khmer Rouge, he come around them and he scream at them. Then he took a small axe and he hit them on the head with the blunt end of the axe and this sound very loud. They have a place for killing there. From far away you can hear the sound of the axe hitting the head. I walk by and know it is happening but there's no scream at all. Imagine that for two years I was there. They put women in drums in the temple and then burn them. They had blood from their eyes and nose. I don't believe it when I speak about it.

'Then we heard on the radio we were being invaded by the Vietnamese. Now we're trapped. The Khmer Rouge give us guns. If we say no, they kill us. I didn't even dare ask how do I use this. Some kids try to run and they got shot. The Khmer Rouge used us as a screen to draw the fire and then we killed countless . . . don't ask me about killing. My friends were killed. Kids cleaning their guns, they blow each other up and intestines coming out.

'I ran off and live in the jungle alone. I had to survive on leaves and trees and after a while I can identify some of the leaves and fruits I can eat. Some kind would poison you and you die. One time my skin fall off because I ate some poison fruit. One time I see a tree with this big fruit like apple all over. I was hungry. I run and pick one. A nice one, a smooth one and I bite it and inside all maggots. I survive mostly by monkey. I lie down on tree and sleep and I wake up, monkeys jumping around. They're always together. Inside I feel so jealous. The small babies they're nice, the baby with the mother. A lot of time it gave me hope. I kept thinking some day I'm gonna see my mother somewhere. . . . I'm learning to cry about it.'

NAVI PILLAY

The daughter of a bus driver and one of seven children, Navi Pillay grew up in Durban, South Africa. Because she's Indian, Pillay was and is subject to discriminatory apartheid laws but she received scholarships and was, unlike many in her community, given the chance to attend a university in South Africa. She then studied law at Harvard University, where she became the first black South African woman to receive a law degree. Cases she has taken on in South Africa have resulted in extremely important changes concerning the way prisoners are treated while in detention and in jail. Her sense that there were many Indians, blacks and coloured people, who would never have the opportunities she had, led her to want to give something back to those who have not had similar advantages. Pillay's husband, Gaby, is also a lawyer and was detained for five months in the early seventies because he gave $100 to a political movement that was *not* banned by the government. Pillay works within a system that, by most standards, is both arcane and unjust: 'In appearance you have a fair trial but it's the content. You know, whether this would be an offence anywhere else in the world. It's extremely difficult to have anybody acquitted under the security law because the onus of proof is on the accused. And the state has everybody who can say anything about the matter in detention so you don't have any witnesses. Can you imagine if you and I were in a motor accident and you had the power to grab all the witnesses and simply lock them up? Any normal court would clearly say that is unjust. But in our security trials that goes on all the time. You cannot say "look this law is immoral" or "all I was trying to do was to have a meeting — it's my freedom of speech". You can't plead arguments that are set out in the Declaration of Human Rights because the judge would immediately say "that's political". So you can't stand up and say racial discrimination is bad and the whole world condemns it. I can't say this openly in South Africa because the country is under emergency and one of the offences would be to be disloyal to the courts.

'Gaby was held in detention because they wanted him to give evidence against his comrades and they wanted to speak untruths. And of course he wouldn't do that. He was the only one of his comrades who wasn't beaten and it's because I was a lawyer. I just kept going to everybody. Every day I went to the security police and I found out where he was being held — even that basic information you don't usually get. I brought an application before the court where I got affidavits from all the other detainees saying they had been tortured. I was able to bring this application because Gaby had given me power of attorney. Otherwise, I wouldn't have been able to because he is the applicant, even though, when he's in detention, he has access to no one. This is why it had never been done before or since. But I didn't function as a lawyer. I wept and cried and got terribly emotional. The security police would refer to him as The Terrorist, "feeding time for The Terrorist is at four" they'd say. When Gaby got the order resulting from my application, he says he just broke down and cried. And he is such a big, strong fellow. They never came near him and he's sure they were about to.

'It hasn't stopped. You get reports that people are being unlawfully interrogated, to put it at its best. But we never give up. We defend every case to the hilt.'

Born and raised in Durban, South Africa, Sonny Venkathrathnum grew up believing that, as an Indian, he was better than the African native blacks but lesser than the whites. He was taught, according to Hindu principles, to believe in reincarnation and was told by his parents that if he was good in this life he would be white in the next. But going to university with other blacks radically changed his perspective. Soon he was teaching English literature and law at a local university for blacks, educating students about the kinds of freedom that exist in other parts of the world. In 1970, Venkathrathnum was put into detention after raising $400 for a political movement that was *not* banned. He would spend the next thirteen years either in detention, prison or under house arrest. While in detention he was beaten severely for six months. He was then sent to Robben Island where he was held for six years, three cells down from Nelson Mandela. Finally, he was released to serve five years under house arrest. Venkathrathnum returned home to see an eight-year-old son whom he'd never met. Although he is now living in New York City, lecturing at Columbia University, Venkathrathnum will return to South Africa in June, even though it might mean a return to house arrest. His life, which has been defined by his struggle, has no meaning apart from the fight against apartheid: 'I was half murdered in detention. Under the terrorism act, they can keep you in detention indefinitely and nobody can say anything. That's where all the deaths take place because there's no protection. I was picked up one morning and just thrown into a cell. They came back an hour later picked me up bodily and they beat me for hours and hours, no questions asked. This went on and on for six months, with the result that I don't have a middle ear. They broke my ear-drum. They ruptured my hernia. You become totally and utterly dependent on your torturers. If that guy allowed you to sit, you think he must be Jesus Christ. If he allowed you to go to the bathroom when you wanted to — you know

Activists:
Clockwise, from top left:
Scharlette Holdman,
Sonny Venkathrathnum,
Navi Pillay, Veronica De-
Negri

without booting you and making you wet your pants — it was a great favour. There isn't a single thing you could do without their consent. Most times they would make you stand. You couldn't shuffle your feet. I'm lucky I survived. One guy was hung by his feet for 58 hours in a tree in a forest until he started to bleed through his ears. He went out of his mind.

'One month after I was in detention, my youngest son was born and I begged my torturers to tell me about my wife and children. One day they opened the peep-hole and told me "you had a son", closed the door and walked off. But, you know, detention does things to you. When they told me that, I thought "wow, my son's okay". They didn't tell me anything about my wife and all these terrible things ran through my mind. During that time they had to take me to a surgeon because I'd developed a rash from head to toe. The doctor prescribed some pills for me. But I thought they were trying to kill me off, so I hid the pills in cracks in my cell. When I heard

about my wife, thinking my wife was dead, I pulled them out and took a fistful of them. Then I heard my daughter cry "Daddy don't do this." I could have killed myself because I discovered later that they were Valium.

'The greatest thing, when I was released, was to see my son. He was eight years old and I hadn't met him. That was the greatest thing. And the second thing was that when I walked into my home I saw hundreds of greeting cards and I asked my wife where's this from? Then she told me about Amnesty. I was adopted as a prisoner in 1971 but they wouldn't let me receive any letters. My wife told me that when I was arrested my friends were told not to go near her because if they did they would be arrested. So my wife became very isolated, lonely. She was at the end of her wits. She lost me, she lost my friends and she had just had a baby and that was when the letters came from all over the world. Suddenly she felt she belonged to a bigger family. They gave my wife courage and hope. For that I am eternally grateful.'

VERONICA DE-NEGRI

Taught, like so many Chileans, under a repressive regime that she did not support, Veronica De-Negri still does not know what exactly caused Pinochet's secret police to 'disappear' her in 1973. She had been working for the Allende government and had demonstrated against Pinochet, but was never charged with any crime. De-Negri was tortured for months, then released and told to leave her country within two months. She emigrated to the US with her two sons. Years later, her eldest son, Rodrigo Rojas, 18, went back to Chile with a friend, Carmen Gloria Quintana. He was taking photographs of a demonstration in Santiago, when he and his friend were pulled from their van by the military police. The police beat them, then doused them with petrol and set them on fire. The two were dumped in a ditch and left to die. De-Negri flew to Chile, but was thwarted by both Chilean medical and political authorities in her efforts to save her son, who died several days later. Gloria survived!

'I had many different kinds of torture. I went through beatings and electric shock on different parts of my body. They did the submarine, where they fill half of a barrel with water or excrement. It depends, they switch from one to the other. And they ask you a question and, if you don't answer, they push you in. Many people died because their lungs fell apart. I was raped not just with men but also with mice. I never saw the light for over six months. I was held for days in a coffin. I was without food a long time and then they'd feed me a huge amount. Your whole system is messed up. Till today I have problems with my kidneys and my circulatory system. My heart stopped three times in there. Then I was taken to a place that was strictly psychological torture, but there I had light for the first time, through a little teeny window. You see the top of a tree which has a lot of meaning. Or you saw fly a bird, that mean life, freedom, hope.

'Both Rodrigo and Carmen Gloria were beaten. Both kids were doused in gasoline and set on fire. The kids extinguished the flames on their bodies without any help. Both kids were wrapped in blankets and dumped in a military truck and they went 12 miles away and dumped them in a ditch with the idea of them to die. They never counted that the kids wanted to live and would manage to get out of the ditch. They got to a poor community clinic. The only thing they could do for them there was to take their clothes off, and then take them to the hospital. Then you can see the cruelty and sophistication of what they do — that there are good and bad doctors. Immediately Rodrigo arrived at the hospital, one of his lungs was collapsed by the doctor that received him. His chances of life went immediately down. I was allowed into the country for a short time. I'm not afraid of anything, I was there to save the life of my son and that is the only thing I care. It was important that Rodrigo get to the hospital, have his medications, have the lab tests. I was able to see my son the first day. My son was not the person who left me. It was very hard. I felt very stupid there because I was talking, talking and he couldn't talk. He couldn't see me. When they burned them, Carmen Gloria was standing and Rodrigo was on the floor. When the flames started, they burned Carmen Gloria from the ankles up and Rodrigo from the head down. His head was very damaged and his eyes. They were forced to drink the gasoline, so the respiratory system was burned. I was proud of him because I saw him struggling for life. I was allowed to see him the moment when he was dying and it was very hard. I never expected he would die. I was preparing myself for a future to deal with this kid, who would be a handicapped kid, but not for him to die. The only part of him that was not burned were his feet. So I was giving him a massage to his feet to help him to live and the doctor was saying, "Why are you doing this? He's dead." I kept doing it and in my need for him to be alive I started to feel that his feet were more warm. But the truth, he was dead. It was like everything that I did to pull him to life, the government, in different ways, was pulling for him to die. It's been two years and the men who killed Rodrigo are free without any charges.'

THE CONCERTS

MONTREAL

TORONTO

PHILADELPHIA

OAKLAND

LOS ANGELES

SAN JOSÉ

SÃO PAULO

MENDOZA

BUENOS AIRES

Friday, 2 September
Wembley Stadium
London, England

Sunday, 4 September
Monday, 5 September
Palais Omnisports Bercy
Paris, France

Tuesday, 6 September
Népstadion
Budapest, Hungary

Thursday, 8 September
Stadio Communale
Turin, Italy

Saturday, 10 September
Camp Neu
Barcelona, Spain

Tuesday, 13 September
Estadio Nacional
San José, Costa Rica

Thursday, 15 September
Maple Leaf Gardens
Toronto, Canada

Friday, 17 September
Stade Olympique
Montreal, Canada

Monday, 19 September
John F. Kennedy
Philadelphia, Pennsylvania, USA

Wednesday, 21 September
Los Angeles Memorial Coliseum
Los Angeles, California, USA

Friday, 23 September
Oakland Coliseum
Oakland, California, USA

Tuesday, 27 September
Tokyo Dome
Tokyo, Japan

Friday, 30 September
Jawaharlal Nehru Stadium
Delhi, India

Monday, 3 October
Olympiako Stadio
Athens, Greece

Friday, 7 October
New National Sports Stadium
Harare, Zimbabwe

Sunday, 9 October
Stade Houphouet Boigny
Abidjan, Côte d'Ivoire

Wednesday, 12 October
Estadio Palmeiras
São Paulo, Brazil

Friday, 14 October
Estadio Mundialista de Mendoza
Mendoza, Argentina

Saturday, 15 October
Estadio River Plate
Buenos Aires, Argentina

LONDON

It's three in the afternoon, only an hour before showtime, and it looks as if London's notoriously miserable weather is going to take its toll on the first concert of the Human Rights Now! tour. Winds are whipping through the empty Wembley Stadium, and rain is pouring down in sheets. But an hour later, as the clock strikes four, the clouds have cleared, and the sun is shining brightly. Nature, it seems, has given the tour a vote of approval.

At exactly 4.08 p.m. Bruce Springsteen, Sting, Peter Gabriel, Youssou N'Dour and Tracy Chapman stroll on to the stage and launch into a capella version of Bob Marley's 'Get Up, Stand Up'. It looks great but sounds terrible—the artists had almost no time to rehearse the song. Still, a more fitting opener would have been hard to come by.

As the Marley anthem chugs to a close, Sting takes the microphone and introduces the man whom Peter Gabriel would later call 'one of the most incredible singers in the world today'. Youssou N'Dour, the Senegalese pop star, and his band, Super Etoile de Dakar, break into 'Nelson Mandela', his song-story about the imprisoned leader of the African National Congress. The heavily percussive music, with its shifting rhythms and pulsating beat, gets the audience—which at this point fills about two-thirds of the cavernous stadium—on to its feet and dancing.

Up in the Royal Box, the section of stadium seats reserved for visiting celebrities and dignitaries, Jack Healey—the man who turned a crazy dream of a world-wide human-rights tour into reality—is ecstatic. Healey bobs up and down like a man possessed. 'What could be better,' he exclaims. 'Good music and a good cause!'

During the brief intermission, Healey slips backstage. There, he's introduced to Peter Gabriel's mother, who gives him an earful about the fact that her son is due on next: 'I think it's rather improper,' she tells the executive producer, 'that Peter go on before it

Jack Healey rouses the Wembley crowd with the Human Rights Now! message

First impromptu session of 'Get Up, Stand Up'

Dolette McDonald –
Sting's back-up singer

gets dark.' Healey is charmed by her comment, but the show's running order was indeed a matter of much debate. Gabriel's set relies heavily on the use of lights, an effect that loses much of its power in daylight. Yet the show's producers didn't want to 'ghettoize' the two black artists—N'Dour and Tracy Chapman— by having them play back-to-back before all of the ticket-holders had even made their way into the stadium. And, because of their massive popularity, Springsteen and Sting were deemed the two logical headliners. As a result, it was decided that Gabriel should go on second.

Dressed in a white shirt buttoned up to the neck and a black suit jacket, Gabriel opens his set with a new song, 'Of These, Hope', written for the sound-track to the Martin Scorsese film, *The Last Temptation of Christ*. He then dedicates his next song 'Games Without Frontiers' to 'the 40,000 needless casualties in the country of Nicaragua, who failed to have their rights protected'.

Throughout the hour he's onstage, Gabriel addresses the human-rights issue more directly than any of the other artists. Before playing 'Don't Give Up', he tells the audience the song is 'the story of a man faced with the problem of unemployment. If you read the Universal Declaration of Human Rights, you'll see that one of the articles deals with everybody's right to a job.' And prior to his encore, he says, 'This

song was written about a country in which there are daily abuses of human rights. This song was written after a young black leader was found dead in his cell . . . This song is just as relevant today as it was then. This song was written for Steven Biko.'

Tracy Chapman is up next and is undeniably the year's biggest musical phenomenon. Six months ago, she was a total unknown: as the Human Rights Now! tour hit the road, however, she has seen her début album sell nearly 5 million copies around the world, reaching Number One in both Britain and America. In England, at least, Chapman's big break came in this same stadium, during the celebrity-studded birthday bash for Nelson Mandela. It's fitting, then, that today's audience, by now nearly 72,000 strong, pays rapt attention throughout her eight-song set.

Once Chapman's off-stage, the show's five artists are rounded up for an official group photo by Annie Leibovitz. Minutes after the shot is done, Sting runs up the ramp to the stage, opening his set with 'King of Pain'. He dedicates the next song, 'If You Love Somebody, Set Them Free', to 'all the children in South African jails'. With noted jazzmen Branford Marsalis on sax and Kenny Kirkland on keyboards, Sting's band is extremely versatile. The highlight is 'They Dance Alone', a song Sting wrote after his experiences during the Conspiracy of Hope tour.

'One of the stories I heard on that tour,' he explained earlier, 'was about the women in Chile, the wives and mothers of those who have "disappeared". They dance as a form of protest, and it struck me as a powerful symbol. It's a non-violent kind of protest, and that appealed to me, because violent protest always invites violent reaction. If anything, the women's dancing invites a kind of stunned awe. It's like saying, "We demand justice, and we have a sense of pride in what we do." So I wanted to amplify what they do and bring it to the attention of the world.'

During the performance, the monitors at the sides of the stage show a video of some of the women dancing at one of Sting's shows in South America. Seeing their faces brings home

LONDON

Gabriel dons a specially
constructed mike in order
to leap about the stage,
simian-style, in 'Shock
the Monkey'

their tragedy. These are real people who have been forced to endure almost unimaginable suffering.

Sting closes with a medley of two old Police numbers 'Bring on the Night' and 'World Running Down', then Peter Gabriel introduces Jack Healey. He exhorts the capacity crowd to work for human rights, and to support the Universal Declaration of Human Rights. His speech is followed by the night's only disappointment: Amnesty officials had commissioned noted-director Stephen R. Johnson, who created Gabriel's 'Sledgehammer' video, to make an animated film about the Universal Declaration, and he, in turn, collaborated with 40 animators from all parts of the world, including the Soviet Union, Poland, Japan and Portugal. The final product, featuring music by Talking Heads leader David Byrne, is both moving and educational. However, at Wembley, a malfunctioning video machine makes it impossible for the fans to hear the soundtrack, and as a result, the video's power is completely diminished.

Even so, the crowd is pumped up and ready when, at nine o'clock, Bruce Springsteen and the E Street Band storm on to the stage and begin blasting out the opening chords to 'Born in the USA'. The set, which lasts a little more than an hour, focuses on the familiar: 'Promised Land', 'Cover Me', 'Cadillac Ranch', 'The River', 'Spare Parts', 'War', 'My Hometown', 'Thunder Road', 'She's the One', 'Light of Day' and a full-blown, electric version of 'Born to Run'. Midway through the set, Springsteen stops to tell the audience how, as a teenager, rock and roll had given him a sense of freedom—and how he feels that Amnesty International does the same thing, on a much larger and more pragmatic scale.

At 10.10 p.m. six hours after the concert's kick-off, Springsteen returns to the stage and calls out Sting, Youssou, Peter and Tracy. Backed by the E Street Band, they launch into another group singalong, this time on Bob Dylan's 'Chimes of Freedom'. Meanwhile, at the side of the stage, Jack Healey hasn't stopped dancing.

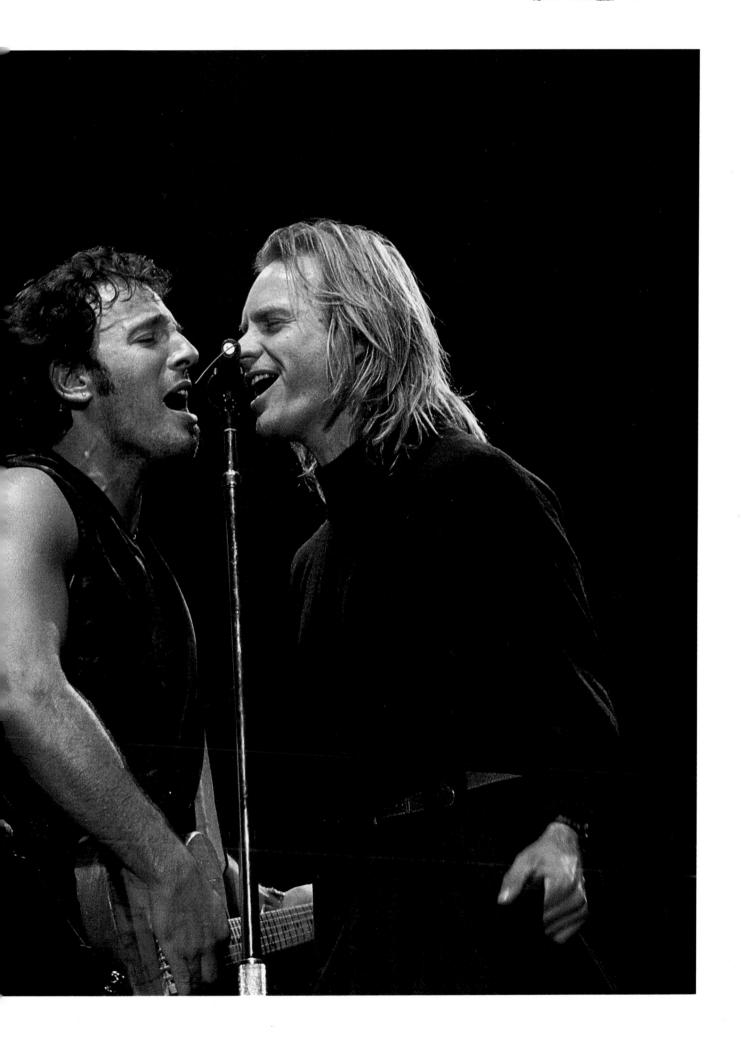

PARIS

Despite the triumphant opening at Wembley and the massive media coverage that came in its wake—virtually every London newspaper raved about the show, and several foreign papers, including almost all major US media, devoted space to the event—several glitches need to be resolved as the Human Rights Now! tour hits Paris, the city where the Universal Declaration of Human Rights was signed in 1948.

For example, only a few hours before the first Paris show, the concert merchandise is nowhere to be found. Tour organizers think it may be locked in a local Reebok warehouse. What's most worrisome, though, is that the passport-sized copies of the Universal Declaration, which Amnesty distributes to the audience at each show, were shipped with the merchandise. The tour organizers could live without the souvenir T-shirts, but on this tour, the Declarations are nearly as important as the music. Fortunately, they arrive at the venue a few minutes before starting-time.

Similarly, the animated video of the Declaration continues to create headaches. On the flight from London, Amnesty officials showed the video on the plane's movie screens—and, once again, it was virtually impossible to hear the sound. Then, during Sunday's show, signals get crossed, and the house lights go up while the video is being aired. This time, the sound is okay but, because the lights are on, the audience fails to grasp the video's significance.

In addition, the running order at the concerts is still a sticky issue. Since the Paris shows are indoors, Peter Gabriel's lighting won't be a problem. But Tracy Chapman was reportedly disturbed that workmen were erecting Sting's set behind her while she was onstage at Wembley, and meetings are held into the early hours of Sunday morning to deal with that.

And those aren't the only problems: Reebok's role is a matter of constant debate. On Sunday, the sportswear company wants to take a group photo of the five artists for a poster, which is to be sold at future concerts. The musicians will agree only if Reebok's name does not appear on the poster. In addition,

Concerts for Human Rights officials are busy trying to work out the details to a proposed live radio broadcast of one of the shows; rights for the tour planes to land in Japan, which somehow got overlooked early on, are being negotiated; and talks are still under way with officials in the Soviet Union, where the tour hopes to stop in less than a month.

Welcome to life on the road.

The two Paris shows are held at a four-year-old, 17,000-seat arena, the Palais Omnisports Bercy. Original plans called for the concert to be at an outdoor race-track that can accommodate 72,000 fans. But new promoters, Gerard Drouot and Michael Deeny, were hired in July, and the show was moved indoors.

The first show kicks off at four on Sunday afternoon with another ensemble rendition of Marley's 'Get Up, Stand Up'. N'Dour, who has a significant following in Paris, then takes the stage to tumultuous applause. He's followed by Michel Jonasz, a major French star whom the local Amnesty section invited to play. Jonasz's music—the kind of romantic, jazz-flavoured ballads that the French adore—

Preparing tour merchandise for sale

Michel Jonasz

**Branford Marsalis – sax
and clarinet, Sting's band**

seems somewhat out of place in this line-up. But his heart is obviously in the right place.

'My songs are about universal love,' he says later, sitting in his dressing-room and smoking a cigarette. 'And that's what this is all about. I often get letters from organizations asking me to take part in these kinds of events. But Amnesty International is the most important one, the one that represents them all. If human rights are respected, all the other organizations won't have to worry.'

Musically, both Paris shows are remarkably better than the London concert. Tracy Chapman, who oddly enough had some doubts about her Wembley set, is ecstatic with her Sunday performance. Her manager calls it one of the best of her career. Peter Gabriel, able to make proper use of his lights, also turns in magnificent performances both nights, while Sting delights the crowd with a version of Jacques Brel's 'Ne Me Quitte Pas' ('Don't Leave Me').

After Sting's Sunday set, Franca Sciuto, the Amnesty chairperson, takes the stage. 'Amnesty International sends many messages to governments,' she tells the crowd in French. 'We don't receive as many messages back from them. But here is one.' She then reads a letter from French President François Mitterrand: 'I salute all of those who have responded to the appeal of Amnesty International, and the artists of all countries who are mobilized in the cause of human rights. Forty years after the United Nations adopted the Universal Declaration of Human Rights, how can we not be struck by the spectacle of a world where the freedom of some people too often serves to suppress the liberty of others. You are here because there remains so much to do to make human rights live. Nothing is ever certain in the struggle for liberty, equality and fraternity. But nothing is ever lost in the persistent work of solidarity. Music can never be contained. It will carry with it throughout this world tour the universal message of human rights.'

Mitterrand's message, while greatly appreciated, causes some debate among the tour organizers. In order to do its work, in a world where human-rights abuses are rampant, Amnesty has a strict policy of impartiality towards all governments and political parties. Every government, no matter how honourable, has the potential to abuse its citizens' rights. By reading Mitterrand's message from the stage the Amnesty officials worry, has the organization set a bad precedent that will make it necessary to read letters from politicians in all nations in which the tour stops, thereby creating a public-relations forum for officials in countries where serious abuses still take place? It's an issue that will take some time to resolve

As at Wembley, the biggest response in Paris is reserved for Bruce Springsteen and the E Street Band. Before playing 'My Hometown', he addresses the crowd in French, once again comparing the freedom he found in rock and roll with the work of Amnesty International and, midway through the show, he asks Sting to join him for a duet on 'The River'.

In the end, what's most remarkable about the tour's initial shows is the degree of enthusiasm and seriousness with which the artists are approaching the concerts. There's no evidence of arrogance or competitiveness, and it's clear that they view the tour as an important commitment and not just a fashionable cause. And that commitment is making itself felt in the music. As tour director Bill Graham says, 'There's good, better and best. Wembley was good. Paris was better. The best is yet to come.' And, indeed, great things do seem to be in store.

Youssou N'Dour and band members, Babacar Faye and Assane Thiam, in a joyous moment

BUDAPEST

Concert goers signing the Declaration of Human Rights petitions

Days like this are the bane of most rock stars' existence. The musicians, many of whom had been out at dinner until 5 in the morning after the second Paris show, have to gather in the lobby of their Paris hotel at 10 a.m., so they can catch an 11 o'clock flight to Budapest. The show there is scheduled to start at 6 p.m. and run until at least 1 in the morning. Then it's back on to the plane for an hour-and-a-half flight to Turin, Italy.

But despite the torturous schedule, this is a day that most of the artists on the Human Rights Now! tour have been waiting for. Tonight's show is the first in somewhat alien territory—and it's the first concert where the human-rights message will take on added political significance.

Upon their arrival in Budapest, the artists meet with about 100 members of the press, including reporters from Bulgaria, Yugoslavia and other Eastern Bloc countries. After making their by-now standard comments about why they are doing the tour—the floor is opened to questions. The reporters' enquiries are the most pointed and intelligent thus far on the tour. Why isn't the tour stopping in Yugoslavia and other Eastern countries?—Time and logistics only

The artists with Janos Brody and Laszlo Foldes, lead singer of Hungary's Hobo Blues Band

permitted one show in the area, explains Bill Graham. What human-rights abuses is Amnesty addressing to Hungary?—Amnesty is working on behalf of nine prisoners of conscience in Hungary, all of whom are in jail because they are conscientious objectors to mandatory military service, Franca Sciuto tells the reporters. What are the political beliefs of Sting, who once said he had been a Marxist in his youth?—'My views have changed a lot since I was 15,' he answers. 'They are very complex, and they sometimes change on a daily basis. I now consider myself a political party of one.' And so on.

During the press conference, Sciuto calls the Budapest show an 'historic moment'. First, the United Nations (UN) Association of Hungary, a voluntary organization that seeks to generate public support for the UN, not only gave its blessing to the show, but also printed 30,000 copies of the Universal Declaration in Hungarian to distribute at the concert. Then, four days before the show, the UN Association invited Ian Martin, Amnesty's Secretary-General, to Budapest. During the visit, Martin met with two representatives of the Hungarian government, the Minister of the Interior and the Deputy Minister of Foreign Affairs. Those meetings signalled a significant breakthrough for Amnesty: not only did they mark the first time an Amnesty representative and an official of an Eastern European government had met face-to-face, but also they opened the door for further negotiations that may enable Amnesty to send its investigative missions into Hungary.

The meetings were widely covered by the Hungarian media, and more than 200 of the country's journalists have subsequently sought credentials for the Human Rights Now! show. In addition, 180 foreign journalists, including ones from the Soviet Union and other Eastern Bloc countries, will also be on hand.

As the six o'clock starting-time approaches, a thunderstorm descends on Budapest. It only lasts a few minutes, then the sun reappears. Outside the stadium, a local football arena called the Népstadion, 80,000 kids—virtually indisting-

Janos Brody, a member of
Illes, Hungary's most
popular rock band in the
sixties

uishable, in their T-shirts and jeans, from rock fans in England and America—have paid the equivalent of about £1.00 to see the show.

Nearby, state-security police casually patrol the grounds. At one booth where copies of the Universal Declaration of Human Rights are being distributed, a policeman picks up the document, scans it, then puts it into his shirt pocket. At another booth, a few fans manage to persuade some officers to sign petitions supporting the Declaration.

Meanwhile, backstage, Laszlo Foldes, the lead singer of Hungary's Hobo Blues Band, is anxiously awaiting this extremely rare opportunity for him to share the stage with the Western superstars. Foldes is widely regarded as one of Hungary's most intellectual rock stars and the band has recorded no less than eight albums. From 1978 to 1982, however, Foldes was banned in 9 of Hungary's 19 counties. And, despite the official sanction that's been bestowed on tonight's show, he's still wary of the government's motives: 'The government will be afraid of us tonight,' he says.

Another Hungarian performer, Janos Brody, will make a surprise appearance at tonight's show. In the sixties, Brody was a member of Illes, Hungary's most popular rock band. In the wake of the Soviet invasion of Prague in 1968, Janos and a fellow member of Illes, Levente Szorenyi, recorded an album dedicated to the Universal Declaration. But during a trip to England, Brody made what the Hungarian government considered inappropriate comments during an interview with the BBC, and when he returned to Hungary, he, too, was banned.

Then, in 1973, Brody wrote a song called 'If I Were a Rose'. Sung to a familiar Hungarian folk-tune, it dealt, indirectly, with repression behind the Iron Curtain. Though it was banned by the government and couldn't be played on radio or TV, the song, because of its familiar melody, became the Hungarian equivalent of 'Blowin' in the Wind'. 'Everyone sang it,' Brody says. 'It was the hymn of the younger generation.' He takes the stage alone, before Sting's set and as he strums his acoustic guitar and sings the words to 'If I Were a Rose', the audience cheers loudly and sings along.

When he leaves the stage, the animated video of the Declaration appears on the screens at the side of the stage, and for the first time on the tour, the audience, which literally packs the stadium to its outer edges, is engrossed.

Backstage, Janos Berecz, a leading member of the Hungarian government, shakes Brody's hand and is introduced to Peter Gabriel. Several other government officials and diplomats, including a key member of the Soviet government, are also in attendance, and both the artists and Amnesty officials are hopeful that the night's concert, which is free of any serious problems or disruptions, will help smooth the way for a show in the Soviet Union. It is clearly the biggest rock-and-roll event ever to take place in Hungary. But as Eva-li Johansson, a reporter covering the concert for Amnesty International's Swedish newsletter, points out, even more exciting than the music is the fact that two words—human rights—seem to have taken on a new meaning behind the Iron Curtain.

TURIN

arty time in Turin. The Human Rights Now! concert is the last big rock-and-roll event of the season, and the Italians are determined to have a blast. Even the city fathers are pitching in: Parco Cavalieri di Vittorio Veneto, a massive park across from Stadio Communale, has been given over to the thousands of kids who have flocked to Turin for the show. Hippies, hustlers and hucksters—they're all here in a bizarre merger of refugees from the Woodstock nation and the tackiest Saturday-morning flea market imaginable. Tents cover the park's interior, while the outer walkway is lined with booths where you can buy everything from incense to political manifestos. And nothing is sacred, not even Amnesty International. Vendors are hawking counterfeit Human Rights Now! posters and T-shirts with a vengeance.

The entourage, which numbers about 200, arrives in Turin at about six o'clock on Wednesday morning. With the exception of the press conference, the artists have the day off, the first time since the start of the tour that they don't have to play a show or travel. Trying to make the most of it, Springsteen heads to the gym for a work-out, Sting plays tennis, Youssou N'Dour hangs out with relatives who live in the city, Tracy Chapman does a little shopping, and Peter Grabriel rents a car and heads off into the mountains for a night away from the tour.

Thursday morning, Chapman's manager, Elliot Roberts, organizes a basketball game at a nearby gymnasium. Roberts, Chapman and Bill Graham win three straight games, soundly beating a team made up of Sting's manager, Miles Copeland, his sax player, Branford Marsalis, and E Street Band guitarist, Nils Lofgren.

Meanwhile, back at the hotels, the tour organizers are trying to plug some holes in the itinerary. Because of slow ticket sales and other logistical problems, one of the two shows planned for Tokyo has been cancelled; in its place, Graham has scheduled a date in Oakland, California, across the bay from his home town of San Francisco.

Another problem exists in India, where the tour hopes to stop on 30 September. *The Times of India*, which had agreed to sponsor the show as part of its 150th anniversary celebration, is squeamish about Amnesty's involvement in

Sting's band members, J.T. Lewis and Branford Marsalis, play their own brand of baseball with crew member, Nico Wormworth

Black-market banners for sale

A table football game featuring Nils Lofgren, E Street Band

the project and has suddenly issued a new dictum: it will not permit any of the organization's officials to take part in the pre-show press conference. Amnesty naturally finds the demand unacceptable. There are also concerns about several other things, including security. But the organizers, believing that the show is one of the most important on the schedule, decide to continue to negotiate in the hope of reaching some compromise, rather than go ahead with a concert in Hong Kong, which had been considered as an alternative.

Meanwhile, the Soviet Union still has not granted permission for the Moscow shows and, suddenly, the tour organizers are faced with the possibility of a week-long gap in the schedule if both Moscow and India fall through. Bill Graham is poring constantly over his world atlas, trying to come up with other suggestions.

As all these negotiations are taking place, 58,000 kids pack the stadium in Turin, cramming up against a barrier in front of the stage more than an hour before the show. In addition to the usual line-up, tonight's concert will also feature the first live appearance in four years by Italian star Claudio Baglioni.

The Turin show marks a home-coming of sorts for Franca Sciuto, the Amnesty chairperson. Back in 1961, when Peter Benenson founded Amnesty, an Italian named Gustavo Comba was one of the first people outside of Britain to organize a local group. After a while, though, the group went into decline. Then, in 1978, Sciuto and two associates re-established the section, and Amnesty now has local offices in several cities around Italy.

For several years, the Italian section had a consistent membership of about 8,000 people. However, in the autumn of 1987, when the Human Rights Now! team was scrambling to raise funds to keep the project alive, the producers of a popular Italian TV show called *Fantastics* offered to contribute its usual artists'

62

Finale with Italian star, Claudio Baglioni

fee of $150,000 if Peter Gabriel or Sting would appear on the show and talk about the tour. A deal was sealed and the show aired a taped interview with Sting, and Gabriel and Sciuto discussed the purpose of the tour.

The response was astounding. Amnesty membership in Italy jumped to 12,000. In addition, during the course of the TV broadcast, Sciuto mentioned that the country's section had never had enough money to publish Amnesty's annual report, which documents human-rights abuses around the world, in Italian. The next morning, several publishers volunteered to print and distribute the 1988 report, which is due to be issued on 5 October, a few weeks after the Turin concert.

Amnesty's success is something of an oddity in Italy. 'Italians are very politicized,' Sciuto explains, 'and it's usually very difficult to make them adhere to a movement that is pragmatic and non-ideological.' Equally important to Sciuto is the fact that the Italian section is based entirely on volunteer work. 'The membership has been reluctant ideologically to create any professional staff positions,' she says. A lawyer by profession, Sciuto herself has done everything from stuffing envelopes and serving as the section's press officer to coordinating the section's work against the death penalty and acting as director of the Milan office.

A CONCERT FOR

HUMAN RIGHTS NOW!

SABADO 10 SEPTIEMBRE 20 HORAS
NOU CAMP- BARCELONA

ENTRADA

Nº 88700

CONTROL 2

BARCELONA

Keeping the fans happy in Barcelona

In the bar of the Ramada Renaissance Hotel, Bruce Springsteen is greeted by two acquaintances he met a month earlier, when his Tunnel of Love tour stopped in Barcelona. Yves Sinclair and his wife supply Barcelona shops and restaurants with home-made pâté, and they've brought several pounds of their speciality here to the hotel as a gift for Springsteen. As he samples the pâté, Bruce waxes enthusiastic about the first week of the tour. 'My band's happier than they've been in years,' he says. 'One of the reasons I did this tour was because I wanted to work with other artists. I haven't toured with any other bands since I was 24 years old, At first, we couldn't get tours with other bands. Then, we got one with Chicago, and it didn't go well. So we decided to play for the people who wanted to see us. We'd play a club, Then, when more people wanted to see us, we'd play two nights in a club. Then three nights, or four nights. Then we moved up to small theatres.

'The funny thing is that, because I live in New Jersey I don't even get to meet many people who do the same job as I do. So I wanted to do that, I wanted to work in a collective of some sort, I wanted to collaborate. I wanted to get in with a bunch of people who had an idea and subsume my identity, into that idea, into that collective, and try to come out with something that's more meaningful and bigger and better than I could on my own. And so far, it's been great.'

Prior to this tour, Springsteen adds, he led a relatively controlled life. He hung out with a small group of people and wasn't very accessible to the outside world, doing few interviews and virtually no press conferences. But that is changing. 'When you're young, you sometimes need that control,' he says. 'But, when you get older, you realize that kind of control isn't good. In rock and roll, you work in a very isolated environment. It seems to come with the nature of the job. And you tend to tour in an isolated environment. You move from town to town, but you're basically with the same group of about 30 people. You try to interact with the communities where you play as much

as you can, but, still, you're only there for a night. It's going to be fleeting.

'I wanted to look outward. Amnesty is international in its appeal, and I like the idea of reaching out to the world community. In the United States, I think, one of the most important things that has to happen is for people to establish some sort of world consciousness. Growing up in the States—certainly during my generation—you felt very disembodied from the rest of the world. The national chauvinism was so great that it encouraged that distance. The first time I came to Europe, in 1981, it was a revelation to me. People live so close together, they have a whole different view on things. A different set of problems, a different view of the world.

'I remember being in London. It seemed like there was so much less violence in the air there. I felt bad, and I wondered why there was such a level of brutality in the US. And I realized that if everybody could just spend some time in Europe when they were 16 or 17, it would change the way people see the world in general. So the idea of working with Amnesty, which promotes a world consciousness, was something that I really wanted to do.'

Across the bar, Sting is equally enthusiastic about the tour. 'I think people are going to be talking about this tour for years to come,' he says, sipping from a glass of mineral water. 'Even people who weren't here will say they were. I think this really is going to be viewed as an historical event.'

For the Spanish section of Amnesty, this tour is a momentous event, which is why the section's leadership fought long and hard for a show in Barcelona. Formed in 1977, the section has 5,000 members in 53 local groups. 'We are a growing section,' Carmen Soto, the chairperson of the section, explains, 'and that is why we thought it would be very important for us to have this concert. We insisted that we have the concert.

'After Franco died, freedom exploded and there were lots of problems,' she continues. 'Working in a democracy is difficult. We weren't used to it. And Amnesty International

Drying out the drums

Sting directs the Boss

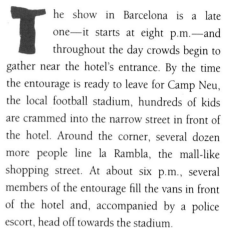

The show in Barcelona is a late one—it starts at eight p.m.—and throughout the day crowds begin to gather near the hotel's entrance. By the time the entourage is ready to leave for Camp Neu, the local football stadium, hundreds of kids are crammed into the narrow street in front of the hotel. Around the corner, several dozen more people line la Rambla, the mall-like shopping street. At about six p.m., several members of the entourage fill the vans in front of the hotel and, accompanied by a police escort, head off towards the stadium.

If the Turin show was wild, this one is pure mayhem. Benefiting from their first sound-check of the tour, and from their first appearance after dark, Youssou N'Dour and his band play their strongest set yet and, fittingly, receive their biggest ovation. El Ultimo de la Fila, a local band whose name translates as the End of the Line, also gets an enthusiastic response, as the stadium literally vibrates from the cheers of the capacity crowd.

Prior to his set, Sting sits down with Veronica De-Negri, one of five human-rights activists who are accompanying the tour from city to city. Tomorrow marks the 15th anniversary of the coup that put General Augusto Pinochet into power in Chile, and De-Negri is one of several thousand people who have suffered under his regime. Seized while providing support for families of political prisoners in Chile, De-Negri survived 'disappearance' and torture, before being released into exile. Then, in 1986, her son Rodrigo returned to Chile to explore his roots. While taking photographs with his friend, Carmen Quintana, Rodrigo was doused with petrol, set afire and left to die.

Because of De-Negri's experiences, Sting has asked her to help him write a statement, in Spanish, which he will read to the audience before 'They Dance Alone', his song about the mothers of the disappeared. 'Tomorrow,' Sting tells the crowd, 'it will have been 15 years since the destruction of the Chilean democracy. Since that day, we have seen brutal arrests, disappearances, decapitations, and young people burned to death in the streets. And the list goes on. The Chilean people deserve a demo-

played a very important role, because it taught us how to respect each other and how to work with someone who may not have the same beliefs. And so this concert is very, very important. It's the first time many young people have learned about the Universal Declaration of Human Rights, and I think it will be very good for the future.'

Based on the media coverage, Soto is not exaggerating the importance that is being placed on this concert. On Friday night, a television commentator calls the show the most significant human-rights event in Spain since the death of Franco. And *El País*, one of Spain's major daily newspapers, hails the tour as a 'splendid feast' and emphasizes its importance in spreading human-rights awareness in the world.

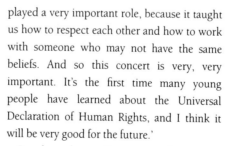

BARCELONA

cratic leader who doesn't have the blood of his own people on his hands.' The audience roars in agreement, then Gabriel joins Sting onstage to perform the song. Thousands of copies of the lyrics were distributed to the audience, which jubilantly joins in. Later, Gabriel draws a similar reaction when, during 'Biko', thousands in the audience light the darkened stadium as they hold matches, cigarette-lighters and candles aloft.

I t was really passionate,' Gabriel says the next day. 'They felt the issue. I think that if the voice of the people can be turned up loud enough, governments can be made to respond, especially if that voice

Marietou Kote – Youssou N'Dour's dancer

An overwhelming response to Sting's 'They Dance Alone'

El Ultimo de la Fila, local band, whose name translates as the End of the Line

is being built on a world-wide basis. The truth is that all governments are concerned about their international standing, and they can't help but respond to this kind of pressure.'

The show goes on until half past four in the morning. When it's finally over, everyone agrees that the European leg of the tour has been a genuine success. Nearly 350,000 people have seen the shows, and thousands of petitions supporting the Declaration have been collected. As Peter Gabriel says, summing up the feeling of the entire entourage, 'It really does feel like history is being made.'

CONCIERTO EN PRO DE LOS
DERECHOS HUMANOS YA!

HECHO POSIBLE POR LA FUNDACION REEBOK©
PROMOTOR LOCAL VIAJES TIKAL

13 SEPTIEMBRE 1988 A LAS 17:00

ESTADIO NACIONAL — SAN JOSE

GRADERIA SOMBRA
¢ 300.00 ENTRADA GENERAL
EVENTO CULTURAL SIN FINES DE LUCRO

4661

S A N   J O S É

A light moment at the press conference

The flight from Barcelona to San José takes nearly 11 hours, and for the first time the entourage—including musicians, Amnesty officials and crew members—is travelling on one of two DC-10s leased from World Airways. Jamie Radner, a producer of the Human Rights Now! tour, helped negotiate the lease of the planes and has had the extremely difficult job of organizing the tour's finances—and keeping them under control.

According to Radner, the entire cost of the tour is between $20 and $30 million, depending on how one calculates the expenses. Approximately $4 million of that is going towards the charter planes, one of which is being used for cargo. Sound, lighting and video equipment, staging and associated freight cost another $6 million. Other expenses include insurance (about $1 million), salaries ($1 million to pay the crews, back-up musicians and other tour employees), hotels ($1.5 million), campaign costs ($1 million for printing the copies of the Universal Declaration, as well as other brochures, press releases and related materials), miscellaneous entourage expenses ($1 million), and such additional items as security, customs and immigration fees and so on.

Radner, an Amnesty member for more than a decade, began working on the tour in January 1987. That month, he and tour consultant Michael Ahern met at the Ryan Hotel in London, where they put together the first budget, estimating the cost at about $15 million. 'At that point, we realized there would be a significant deficit,' Radner says. 'It was going to cost an enormous amount of money transporting the equipment and the entourage from country to country, and, because we planned to play in out-of-the-way places, we wanted to keep the ticket prices low. So we knew we would have to come up with money from outside sources.' Eventually, Radner and Jack Healey managed to negotiate the deal with Reebok, that gave the Concerts for Human Rights Foundation both the financial guarantee it was seeking, as well as a limit on the amount of commercialization.

Radner had other problems, as well, such as convincing the US government that the tour was a charity project and, as a result, should be granted tax-free status. 'Because of Reebok's involvement, and because it's a rock-and-roll tour the Internal Revenue Service was somewhat suspicious,' he says. 'In order to get the tax status we wanted, we had to convince them that the tour would "educate and uplift".' In the end, Radner accomplished that goal, too.

When the plane lands in San José, several members of the entourage emerge with their heads wrapped in white pillowcases, and it's apparent from the looks on their faces that the Costa-Rican customs officials have never had to deal with a group quite like this one.

In fact, the Human Rights Now! caravan is the first major Western rock tour to hit these shores since 1971, when Santana appeared in San José. And though the government of President Oscar Arias has welcomed the tour, inviting the artists to a private meeting at his office, the Catholic archbishop of San José spared no words in condemning the concert, saying it would encourage the use of drugs, a major concern in Costa Rica.

When the artists meet with the President on Monday afternoon, Sting brings up the archbishop's criticisms. 'Well,' responds Arias, 'he was only worried because we have no army, no police, just a few civilian guards. We are a very open society. Our territory has been used for the trafficking of drugs, and we are worried that it is becoming one of the main issues in our internal political life.'

The meeting with Arias is awkward at best. Quiet and seemingly distracted, Arias begins by admitting that he knows little about rock and roll. In fact, he says, he doesn't really

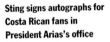

Sting signs autographs for Costa Rican fans in President Arias's office

understand why the tour has stopped in his country. He then launches into a low-key speech about Costa Rica. As Arias explains, Costa Rica is an island of peace and relative prosperity in a region torn by war and poverty. The country outlawed the death penalty a century ago, and it abolished its army in 1949, converting the barracks into schools and rechannelling defence funds into education and social-welfare programmes. 'Our main defence', Arias tells the artists, 'is to be defenceless . . . We don't have any tanks, any helicopters, or any machine-guns.'

Indeed, there are rarely reports of human-rights abuses in Costa Rica, and Arias himself was awarded the Nobel Peace Prize for his widely hailed Central American peace plan. In addition, San José is the home of the University for Peace, an organization Peter Gabriel has been closely involved with. 'The basic goal is peace through education,' Gabriel says. 'The idea is to make peace as much a part of daily education as war is.'

After about twenty minutes, the meeting adjourns, and Arias asks if the artists would mind posing for some photos with his children

Fans undeterred by the tail end of Hurricane Gilbert

and the children of his staff, who have filled an adjacent office. The artists agree, though they are surprised by the throng that awaits them. It's even worse outside, where the number of photographers and fans has doubled since the start of the meeting. The scene is reminiscent of nothing so much as the heyday of Beatlemania, as screaming girls surround the vans, making it simply impossible for the musicians to get back on board. Fortunately, no one is hurt in the mêlée, but afterwards, at a press conference back at the hotel, one journalist charges that he was kicked by a security man, and the artists agree to investigate the allegation, which turns out to be groundless.

On Tuesday, the day of the show, torrents of rain brought on by Hurricane Gilbert pelt the city and, for a while, it seems doubtful that the concert, which is being held at an outdoor football stadium, will be able to go on. But despite the archbishop's warning, the youth of Costa Rica are obviously excited by the prospect of the show, and several thousands of them, undeterred by the downpour, begin gathering outside

**Costa Rican singer,
Guadaloupe Urbina**

the stadium early in the day.

The rain eventually lets up and, at five o'clock, the concert gets under way as scheduled. Estadio Nacional—which looks more like a high-school football field than a major national sports stadium—is soaked from the rain, its field a sea of mud. Still, the stadium is roughly three-quarters full, with a total attendance of approximately 30,000 including several busloads of fans from all over Central America, as well as about 60 US Peace Corps volunteers who are stationed in Costa Rica.

Despite President Arias' claims about his country's peaceful environment, it's obvious that this is not nirvana. About 300 armed civilian security guards patrol the stadium, and though official reports later claim that only five people are arrested during the course of the show, witnesses report seeing many more confrontations between the police and fans.

The show is an incredible success, and the audience, drenched by regular downpours throughout the evening, stays until the very end. The next day, the newspapers feature the concert prominently on their front pages, giving it as much coverage as Hurricane Gilbert. Peter Gabriel is ecstatic about the symbolic importance of the

show. 'I'd love to see an independent Central America that didn't have to rely on the US, Cuba, or the Soviet Union,' says Gabriel, an ardent critic of America's policy in the region. 'Somehow, in America, foreign policy has gotten caught up with masculinity. That policy is fed by ignorance, and it only works if there is a distance between people, if you can create an enemy by depersonalizing someone who doesn't agree with you. It's very easy to turn nationalism into racism, and that destroys human rights faster than anything. Anything that can reduce that distance—which is what this tour is trying to do—should be encouraged.'

**Sting with bassist, Tracy
Wormworth**

15 SEPTEMBER · MAPLE LEAF GARDENS · TORONTO · CANADA

TORONTO

The news today is not good. Negotiations with the Soviet Union have stalled, and it now appears that it will be impossible for the tour to stop there in early October, as planned. Though no official word has come from the Soviet government, one of the nation's more conservative leaders is reportedly against the concert, and despite several overtures by friendly politicians, artists and journalists, Amnesty has been unable to win approval.

Even so, the tour organizers aren't giving up, and there's a slight hope that a breakthrough might still be possible. If that happens, the show would be added at the end of the tour, after the 15 October concert in Buenos Aires. Meanwhile, Peter Gabriel, ever the optimist, offers an unlikely alternative, suggesting that the tour's plane make an unscheduled refuelling stop in Moscow, during which the artists would hold an impromptu press conference at the airport.

Difficulties with *The Times of India* also continue to plague the tour organizers. Almost every day, the newspaper, which is to sponsor the show in New Delhi, throws up a new road-block. The matter of Amnesty representation at the pre-concert press conference was resolved when Indian officials said they would allow Jack Healey, the head of the Concerts for Human Rights Foundation and the Executive Director of Amnesty International USA, to be present. Now, however, two more issues are threatening the show. One involves the number of people who would be allowed to sit on the field during the concert. The Indians want to limit the number, creating a situation that the tour organizers fear could result in violence. In addition, *The Times of India* is insisting on much higher ticket prices than the Concerts Foundation wants. As a result, Jamie Radner, Bill Graham and George Travis, one of the tour's main consultants, are on the phone into the wee hours of the morning, trying to resolve the problems.

As the negotiations continue, alternatives are being explored. On the flight from Costa Rica, Graham and Gabriel spend an hour together, discussing the options. Graham, a pragmatist, is advocating a show in Athens, Greece, which could be put together relatively quickly. Gabriel, on the other hand, takes the position that every effort should made to schedule the concerts in areas where the human-rights message will have greater impact. One option is Seoul, South Korea, the site of the summer Olympics. On Thursday morning, Foundation officials make plans to contact the head of the International Olympics Committee to see if such a show would be possible.

Other suggestions include Senegal, the home of Youssou N'Dour. The African nation had been on the original itinerary, but a curfew was imposed after presidential elections there, so the concert was switched to the Côte d'Ivoire. The curfew has since been lifted, and the organizers consider asking N'Dour to contact Senegal's president. Indonesia, Turkey, Yugoslavia and Poland are also considered. 'There will never be another tour like this,' Graham says with a chuckle. 'I mean, would you have believed that we'd be sitting here with an atlas, trying to figure out what country we'll be playing in two weeks?'

After the ecstatic responses in Europe and Costa Rica, the Toronto show is something of a let-down. The concert is held at the 16,000-seat Maple Leaf Gardens, a rickety, decrepit indoor arena that seems almost like a night-club when compared to the open-air stadiums in Barcelona and Budapest. Unfortunately, that relative intimacy doesn't translate into a wild reception, and

K. D. Lang and band, recent winners of the Canadian Country Music Awards

TORONTO

during the early performances, the fans are fairly subdued. One highlight, however, is the set by K. D. Lang, a Canadian singer who in the last year has become a country-music sensation. Lang, who mixes good old country music with the aggressiveness of punk, was a last-minute addition to the bill, after Bryan Adams bowed out because of a recording commitment. A resident of Vancouver, in western Canada, Lang had spent the weekend in Toronto, where she and her band swept the Canadian Country Music Awards. She returned home on Monday, only to get a call inviting her to appear at the show.

'There was no question that we'd do it,' she says after her set. 'We turned right around and came back to Toronto.' As it turned out, she was a smart addition to the bill. 'I'm very humanistically aware,' she says. 'What this tour is all about is education. We're so sheltered in Canada and the US that we need organizations like Amnesty to bring attention to the injustices in the world. I'm sure a lot of these people have just come to see Sting and Springsteen, but in the stir that the whole tour causes, issues are brought up, and the aware-

ness really does rocket.'

By the end of the night, though, it was apparent that most of the fans had come to see Springsteen, who bypassed Toronto on his last tour. As Craig MacInnis, a critic for the *Toronto Star*, wrote the next day, 'If last night's Amnesty International benefit left one lasting impression—apart from the need to protect civil liberties and freedom of expression—it was that Springsteen can do no wrong. The Jersey superstar bounded into the spotlight near the stroke of midnight—and suddenly, it was an entirely different concert.'

MONTREAL

f Toronto was something of a disappointment, Montreal turns out to be a splendid surprise. From Friday evening when a joint press conference is held with both the French- and English-speaking Canadian sections of Amnesty, through Saturday night's show at Olympic Stadium, the city literally vibrates from the enthusiasm generated by the concert's human-rights message.

The press conference is one of the more invigorating of the tour. Peter Gabriel and Sting deliver their speeches in French, the official language of the Province of Quebec, while Bruce Springsteen apologizes for his lack of fluency in the language: 'Excusez-moi, je ne parle pas français,' he reads from a slip of paper. Unfortunately, the interpreters, unable to hear the artists, also have some problems with the translations, and more than once, Gabriel has to correct them.

Springsteen, Sting, Gabriel, Tracy Chapman and Youssou N'Dour are joined at the conference by Daniel Lavoie and Michel Rivard, the two local artists enlisted for the Montreal show. Both prove to be articulate spokesmen for Amnesty.

During the question-and-answer period, a reporter asks about Canada's human-rights record. 'Your record is a long way from a just one,' Gabriel responds. 'But there are many worse countries.' In particular, he cites proposed legislation that would put restrictions on refugees seeking shelter in the country. 'Canada has a reputation as an excellent haven for refugees who have suffered, but the new laws would make it harder for them to enter the country,' Gabriel says. On the other hand, he praises the country for its long-term stand against the death penalty.

Chilean relatives of the 'disappeared' present Sting with a poncho, in gratitude for his song 'They Dance Alone'

hile the musicians field about a dozen other questions, one member of the audience, a slight, elderly man, pays close attention. Forty years ago, that man, John Humphreys, wrote the first draft of the Universal Declaration of Human Rights. 'I've never pretended to be the father of the Declaration,' says Humphreys, now a professor at McGill University in Montreal. 'I prepared the draft, but in doing so, I referred to several

¡Olé!

**Montreal performer,
Michel Rivard**

**Daniel Lavoie, local
Montreal artist, gets into
role for his song**

other drafts written by hundreds of other people. Even H.G. Wells contributed to it.'

The job of writing the draft, says Humphreys, was not a particularly difficult one. 'The issues are pretty fundamental. We all know what torture is, and that it should be abolished. And we know the importance of freedom of speech.' What did surprise many people, though, was the inclusion of the social and economic rights. 'That's the extraordinary aspect of the Declaration,' Humphreys says. 'For the first time at the international level, there was some recognition of the existence of those rights. The conventional wisdom is that they were put into the Declaration by the USSR. But that's just hogwash. The reason they're there is because human rights don't mean a thing if you have an empty stomach.'

In retrospect, Humphreys, who spent 20 years at the human-rights division of the United Nations, believes the Declaration has more than served its purpose. 'It's turned out to be more important than anyone realized. It's been invoked so many times that it's now recognized as part of the customary law of nations.' And while he confesses that he's 'not particularly' a fan of rock music, Humphreys is none the less enthusiastic about the Human Rights Now! tour. 'I think it's an excellent thing they're doing. We have no mechanisms to enforce the implementation of human rights at the international level. So the only thing we can really do is educate public opinion. All governments are sensitive to public opinion. Even totalitarian governments. That's why something like this is so important.'

On Saturday morning, several members of the entourage take a 20-minute drive to the outskirts of Montreal, where about 5,600 members of the Mohawk nation, a tribe of native North-American Indians, live on a 14,000-acre settle-ment. A representative of the Mohawk had shown up at Friday's press conference to greet the artists. 'The Chiefs, Clan Mothers and people of the Mohawk nation at Kahnawake wish to welcome you to our territory. We understand the situation that many native people face today, as our community is bracing for another invasion by Canadian paramilitary forces.'

In June, Royal Canadian Mounted Police raided the settlement at Kahnawake, seizing money and tobacco products, which the members of the tribe import and distribute in an effort to raise money for the tribe. At issue is the Mohawks' attempt to attain economic self-sufficiency and to retain sovereignty over their territory. 'We are trying to show what you can do if you take control,' Earl Cross, a spokesman for the tribe, tells the Human Rights Now! delegation. 'If we allow the Canadian government to push us around, they will take away our culture. What they want are good Canadians. We want to keep our traditions, yet stay in touch with the reality of the times.'

While that meeting is taking place, some 1,500 high-school students have gathered in Parc Lafontaine for what's being called the March of the New Generation for Human Rights. Organized by the French-speaking section of Amnesty and a national teachers union, the event kicks off with speeches by former prisoners of conscience. Dressed in his native garb, Roger Urbain tells the crowd of the dreadful conditions he endured during his imprisonment in Benin, a country in West Africa. Fifteen people were held in one cell. A hole in the floor served as the toilet. Partway through his internment, he says, he contracted a disease that caused him to cough up blood. Still, he was refused medical treatment.

Patti Scialfa – Bruce Springsteen's back-up singer

Nils Lofgren on stage

'Thanks to Amnesty International, and everyone who supports Amnesty International, I was finally released and flown to Quebec, where I received treatment from doctors associated with Amnesty International,' Urbain says. 'A small thing like writing a letter can make a difference.'

Franca Sciuto then takes Urbain's hand, and the hand of a former prisoner from Zaire. 'This is Amnesty International,' she says. 'This is what our movement means. And you are Amnesty International.'

After the speeches, the students assemble for a two-hour march to Olympic Stadium. Leading the procession is a flat-bed truck, on the back of which are several cages holding 'prisoners' pulled from the crowd by students dressed in military uniforms. When they arrive at the stadium, the 'prisoners' are released, along with several hundred white balloons. Afterward, Sciuto is delighted. 'We've had wonderful experiences in Europe and Central America, but this is the first time that young people have actually organized to show that they support the real meaning of this tour.'

A near-capacity crowd of 60,000 people have shown up for the concert, although the stadium is so huge that it looks as if another 10,000 people could fit inside quite comfortably. While Tracy Chapman is onstage, a group of Chilean refugee women who live in Montreal come backstage to meet Sting. They present him with a poncho, made by relatives of the 'disappeared', as a gift of thanks for his song 'They Dance Alone'. One of the women, Ximena Campos, tells of her brother, Eduardo, who disappeared on 13 September 1973. 'As a family, we disintegrated after the coup,' she tells Sting. Eduardo, a car mechanic who was planning to study engineering at Santa Maria University in Valparaiso, committed no crime that his sister is aware of. 'It was a military strategy to go out and kill,' she says. 'The streets were full of bodies. Bodies were flowing down the river in Santiago. We were scared to death. No one ever believed the military would do this. The government says they are defending democracy, but they should be exercising it.'

'They Dance Alone', she says, has given her and many women, both in and out of Chile, some comfort. 'I was overwhelmed when I heard it. I was so moved, I cried.'

The show, which lasts until nearly two a.m., closes with Springsteen's hour-and-fifteen-minute set of blood-curdling rock and roll. Earlier, at the press conference, one reporter asked why he had been concentrating on such up-tempo material. 'I felt my job on the Amnesty tour,' Bruce replied, 'was to come out at the end of the night and rock the house.' And, after nine shows, it's clear that he takes that job quite seriously.

PHILADELPHIA

In-flight fight

Buoyed from the reception it received in Montreal, the Human Rights Now! tour picks up even more momentum as it arrives in Philadelphia for the first US concert date. On Sunday, the day before the show, the *Philadelphia Inquirer*, one of America's most respected newspapers, runs a front-page story on Amnesty's Urgent Action Network, a world-wide telecommunications system that aids people in immediate and extreme danger. In addition, the paper publishes stories about the tour on the front pages of both its Business and its Entertainment sections.

Sunday morning, about 400 people show up for a rally on Independence Mall. According to a report in the *Inquirer*, American actress Margot Kidder tells the gathering that 'we must accept our place in the human family. We must lead our leaders. We must teach them respect for human life.' The rally also features speeches by former prisoners of conscience from Kampuchea (Cambodia), South Africa and Argentina.

'I myself experienced torture like you saw in the movie *The Killing Fields*,' says 43-year-old Kassie S. Neou, who was arrested in Cambodia and accused of working for the CIA. 'The young soldiers, to some extent, were just having fun, beating me. All I saw was torture

and killing and rape.' While in a refugee camp in Thailand, Neou wrote to Amnesty, asking the organization to help stop the Cambodian genocide. 'They saved not only me, but thousands of others.'

'The courage that has been displayed by Amnesty International has given some people something to live for,' adds Nomgcobo Sangweni. 'For when you're in jail in South Africa, you are not human, you are just a number. And when the letters start coming in, you know someone does care about you.'

Monday morning, the *Inquirer* continues its saturation coverage of the tour. A page-one story by staff writer Dick Polman deals with rock and roll's increasing involvement in politics, while nearly two full pages of the Entertainment section are devoted to the Human Rights Now! caravan, including a lengthy profile of executive producer Jack Healey. More so than any other newspaper or magazine, the *Inquirer* seems to have captured the meaning and spirit of the tour.

At noon on Monday, about 300 reporters and photographers—including journalists from America's three major TV networks and most of the country's important newspapers—assemble in the Grand Ballroom at the Four Seasons Hotel.

Get up, stand up!

**Tracy Chapman joins
Peter Gabriel in 'Don't
Give Up'**

Long-time activist and singer Joan Baez, who will appear at the three US shows, kicks off the artists' comments by telling the story of a woman she met some 15 years ago, when she first started working for Amnesty.

'This woman had been in the resistance in France and Italy, long before the Universal Declaration of Human Rights had been written and many, many years·before Amnesty had been dreamed of. So when she was imprisoned and tortured, and left for lost in a black cell, she said what so many prisoners have said to me, which is that the worst thing for them is the sense that everybody has forgotten that they exist. That is the real terror—that they've been forgotten and that nobody cares about them. And this woman was in her cell, with these feelings of despair, when someone passed her a note that said "Couragio"—courage. And at that point, she knew that not only was she remembered, but that people on the outside were working for her. It was the rebirth of hope, and hope is the essential ingredient needed to revive the human spirit.'

A significant portion of the press conference is devoted to a critique of America's role in human-rights abuses around the world. In his opening remarks, Healey calls on President Reagan 'to remove not only the missiles from the world, but to remove torture from our allies, to remove killings and disappearances. The United States must bring all of our allies to the table of justice and look them in the eye and demand justice from them. . . . Let's restore the sense of hope that the signers of the Universal Declaration brought to this world of ours 40 years ago.'

During the question-and-answer period, Bruce Springsteen echoes Healey's remarks. 'It doesn't seem that, as a nation, we are out there in the forefront, leading the world in human-rights policy. And I don't believe that, in that sense, our foreign policy reflects the basic decency that I still believe the American people have. So . . . get on the job!'

With equal urgency, Healey and the artists call for the abolition of the death penalty in the States. 'We believe deeply that the death penalty is an abhorrent abuse of human rights, and we intend to defeat it,' Healey says. 'If this

Bruce Springsteen with E Street Band member, Clarence Clemons

country thinks it can continue the death penalty, and, at the same time, still lead the world, it's mistaken.'

'What this country has created,' adds Peter Gabriel, 'is a twentieth-century version of human sacrifice.'

Midway through the press conference, a telegram arrives from the US Consulate in South Africa. In it, three South African activists who escaped detention and took refuge in the consulate state their determination to remain there 'until reasonable guarantees of our freedom are obtained'. They then thank the Amnesty groups that have adopted them as prisoners of conscience and offer their best wishes for success to the tour.

Throughout the conference, Sting winds up being the butt of some good-natured teasing from the other artists. Asked if the musicians are teaching each other about the situations in their own countries, Tracy Chapman says, 'What can we teach Sting that he doesn't already know?' Adds Springsteen: 'Sting once said he knew every answer to every question.' And, later, Bruce adds, 'In between sets, Sting tutors me on what's wrong with my music.'

About a half-hour away, JFK Stadium is turning into a madhouse. Not only have some 75,000 fans turned out for the show, but hundreds of media people and celebrities. At about five o'clock, after the ensemble opening of 'Get Up, Stand Up', Joan Baez takes the stage to sing 'Oh, Freedom' and

PHILADELPHIA

**Springsteen and Sting
harmonize 'The River'**

John Lennon's 'Imagine'. Despite the back-stage mob scene, the show runs smoothly and on time. The high point of the evening comes during Gabriel's set, when Tracy Chapman joins him for 'Don't Give Up'. As critic Tom Moon writes in the next day's *Philadelphia Inquirer*, 'Bending her voice to fit the twisting, gospel-influenced lines, Chapman sounded at ease and reassuring.'

When Springsteen takes the stage, he's backed for the first time on this tour by the horn section that accompanied him during his Tunnel of Love shows. And, saying 'We're gonna do something that we haven't done in a long time, just for Philadelphia,' he plays 'Jungleland', one of his early anthems.

On Tuesday morning, the *Inquirer* once again devotes considerable space to the concert, including two stories on page one. There's no question that the two-day visit was a success, in terms of both awareness and music. As Tom Moon writes, 'Surprisingly, throughout the marathon, there were moments in which the message and the music magically coalesced. If the stadium mega-event has become synonomous with blunt bashing and little musical communication, this concert ... showed that subtlety is not only possible, but desirable.'

LOS ANGELES

Bono and wife, Alison

Itinerary update: India is on, and so is Athens, Greece. Bill Graham has flown to New Delhi to co-ordinate arrangements for the show there. The Athens concert will be held in a 70,000-seat stadium, and there's still a slight chance that another date will be added on 5 October, two days before the show in Harare, Zimbabwe.

Medical update: With India now on the schedule, Jerry Fox, the tour's nurse and resident medical expert, has his work cut out for him. In other words, it's innoculation time on the Human Rights Now! tour. And, on Tuesday morning, Fox's room is transformed into a mini-medical centre, as he and a local doctor administer shots to wary musicians, managers and human-rights activists.

The reception in Los Angeles is expected to be mixed, at best. When the concert was announced, with a starting time of two in the afternoon on Yom Kippur, the Jewish holiday, a storm of protest blew up in local media and music circles. Eventually, the showtime was changed to seven p.m., after sunset, the official end of the holiday. But the damage was done, and ticket sales never approached the number initially anticipated.

Still, it's unlikely that the slow ticket sales can be blamed entirely on the Yom Kippur fiasco, and managers and other tour personnel also point to the fact that both Springsteen and Sting played in the area earlier this year, lessening the appeal of the Amnesty bill. Another reason frequently cited is 'benefit fatigue'. According to that theory, rock fans, particularly in America, are tired of star-studded shows and prefer to see their favourite artists in a solo setting.

**Ellen Bernstein and
Barbra Streisand**

When the show gets under way, the Coliseum looks virtually empty, with just a smattering of fans on the field and in the pastel-coloured grandstands. By the time Tracy Chapman takes the stage, after Youssou N'Dour's set and Joan Baez's opener, it is starting to fill up. The almost painfully shy Chapman introduces 'Freedom Now', her song inspired by Nelson Mandela, with a story: 'I was talking to someone earlier, and he asked me, "Who are you raising money for?" And I said, "We're not raising money for anyone." And he said, "Oh, you mean you're raising money for yourself?" And I told him no, that I wasn't even being paid. And he said, "Well, then, what are you doing this for?" And I told him we were trying to raise people's awareness about the issue of human rights, and about the Universal Declaration of Human Rights, which I hope all of you have copies of.' The audience roars. 'And we're trying to do this,'Chapman continues,'in the hope that if we're aware of our own rights, and we work to

Sting and John Dukakis

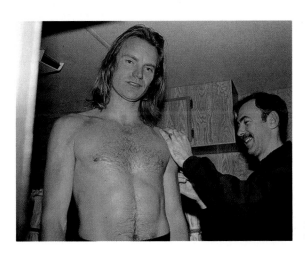

**Sting gets innoculated
for India**

make our governments enforce those rights, then someday we'll live in a better world than we have now.'

During 'Baby Can I Hold You', Branford Marsalis comes onstage to embroider Chapman's vocal and guitar lines with his distinctively elegant sax stylings, much to the audience's delight. As the tour has progressed, Chapman's passionate vocals and strong, dignified stage presence continue to entrance the crowds, no easy accomplishment in stadium settings far more conducive to Peter Gabriel's more theatrical presentation or Bruce Springsteen's no-holds-barred rock and roll.

Despite the disappointing turn-out, the scene backstage, though far more orderly than in Philadelphia, is like a who's who of LA celebrities. Two members of U2, Bono and Larry Mullen Jnr, as well as the group's manager Paul McGuinness, are hanging out in the massive white tents that

serve as the artists' dressing rooms. The band has been in Los Angeles for the better part of the year, working on their new album and movie, *Rattle and Hum*, and, in part, it was that obligation which kept the group from participating in the Human Rights Now! tour. Two other long-time Amnesty boosters, Jackson Browne and Daryl Hannah, also drop by to say hello. Sting, meanwhile, spends a few minutes schmoozing with John Dukakis, the son of presidential candidate Michael Dukakis. Other celebs include Barbra Streisand, Debra Winger, Whoopi Goldberg, Ally Sheedy, Rob Lowe, Michael J. Fox and Jon Bon Jovi.

Back onstage, the artists continue the kind of collaborations that are making this tour a special musical event. Sting joins Peter Gabriel for 'Games Without Frontiers', and, during Springsteen's set, violinist Shankar comes onstage for 'The River', while percussionist Mino Cinelu helps out on 'War'. Prior to 'The River', Bruce introduces Sting by saying, 'I'd

like to bring out the man who's finally convinced me to take a shot at acting. We're planning to do a remake of *Abbott and Costello Go to Mars*.' And before 'My Hometown', Springsteen makes his most passionate plea yet for human rights. 'Human-rights abuses aren't just something that happen a thousand miles away from here,' he tells the crowd. 'When you see a homeless person on the street, human rights are being abused. When someone in this city doesn't have enough food to eat, or enough money, that person's rights are being abused ... So take a stand and join Amnesty International.'

When Springsteen calls everyone back out after his set for the 'Chimes of Freedom' finale, Bono, dressed in a cowboy hat and black coat and pants, joins in. It's another magical moment for Jack Healey, who had been extremely disappointed by U2's inability to take part in the tour. Earlier in the day, Healey injured his back during one of the entourage's by-now regular basketball skirmishes. Though he says he's in a great deal of pain, it doesn't show as he takes up his usual position at the side of the stage and ends the night with a joyous dance.

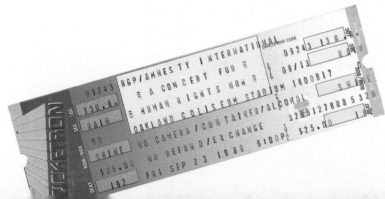

OAKLAND

Life on the road with a rock-and-roll tour isn't all it's cracked up to be, especially not when you're trying to go around the world in 40 days, like the Human Rights Now! caravan is. Airport, bus, hotel, bus, stadium, bus, airport. It all starts looking alike, and just remembering what city you're in can be difficult. As a result, little details that distinguish one place from another start taking on added significance.

Of course, the big details are even more noteworthy, like when the tour arrives in San Francisco and, at the last minute, a decision is made to switch hotels. Because of a union dispute, there's a picket line in front of the hotel where the entourage had planned to stay, and Foundation officials decide it would be inappropriate to cross it. So, on Thursday afternoon, nearly 100 people spend about two hours camping out in the lobby of a different hotel, as new rooms are booked for the band members and Amnesty officials. Not everyone's happy about it, but Jack Healey is adamant: he's not crossing a picket line, period.

Other highlights of the visit to San Francisco include:

- A meeting between the tour's human-rights activists and Bay Area activists. California has the third-highest number of people on death row in the United States, and lawyers from a group called CAP discuss their work against capital punishment. Then, Brian Wilson, a Vietnam vet who now heads an organization called the Institute for the Practice of Non-Violence, tells how a visit to Nicaragua in 1985 radicalized his views on American foreign policy: 'The Contras attacked a village in the mountains where I was living,' Wilson says. 'They tortured and killed five mothers and two children. And I saw my tax money, and it was killing people.' After that experience, Wilson fasted for 47 days on the steps of the US Capitol building, to show the anguish of the Nicaraguans. Then on 1 September 1986, while taking part in a protest against the shipment of armaments in California, Wilson was struck by a train and lost parts of both of his legs. 'Since then,' he tells the group, 'I've been trying to figure out the meaning of my survival.'

- Actress Margot Kidder directing a video intended to introduce the entourage—and, especially, members of the road crew—to the work of the five human-rights activists accompanying the tour. After shooting footage at both the hotel and the Oakland Coliseum, Kidder stays up all night editing the video. When she's done, she gives two video cameras to a hotel bellboy, who places them in

Halfway through the tour, and thousands of miles to go!

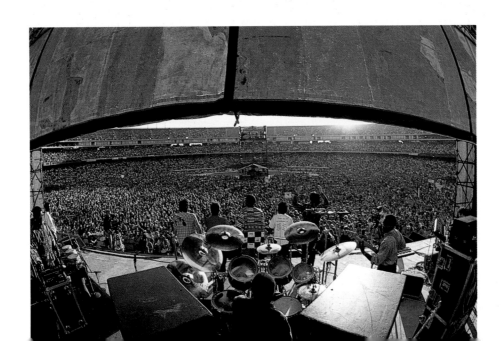

After 'Lay Your Hands on Me', Peter Gabriel makes a spectacular descent into the crowd

OAKLAND

A congratulatory kiss
from Baez to Springsteen
on his birthday

the wrong room. As the entourage heads to the Oakland Airport for the trip to Japan, the tour's next stop, the cameras are missing, and so is the video.

● The selection of Jack Healey as 'Person of the Week', on the ABC-TV evening news. During the piece, the network airs photos of Healey as a child and as a priest, causing Healey to quip, 'I've spent the last 20 years trying to hide the fact that I was a priest, then they go and show pictures of me in my robes on national TV!' In reality, it's a great honour, and Healey's delighted.

● Joan Baez and Bruce Springsteen singing a duet of Bob Dylan's 'Blowin' in the Wind' during her set at the Coliseum. After bringing Bruce out onstage, Baez leads the capacity crowd of 59,000 in singing 'Happy Birthday' to Springsteen, who turned 39 the day of the Oakland concert.

● Rock-legend Roy Orbison hanging out backstage. talking to Springsteen and the other artists.

● The road crew donning T-shirts emblazoned with Article 24 of the Universal Declaration of Human Rights. The article guarantees reasonable limitations of work hours, and the crews—who have been toiling about 20 hours a day—have jokingly started calling Healey 'Mr 24.'

● A longer-than-usual set by Youssou N'Dour. Because of previous commitments, Sting and his band are unable to play in Oakland and, as a result, Youssou stays onstage for nearly an hour and delivers his most exhilarating performance of the tour thus far.

27 SEPTEMBER · TOKYO DOME · TOKYO · JAPAN

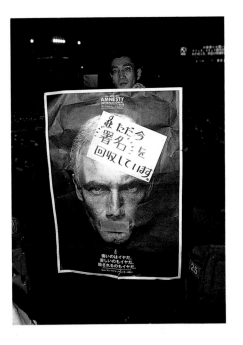

he Emperor is dying, and everyone in Japan—including the members of the Human Rights Now! entourage—is keeping a close watch on his condition. The media here give regular updates on his health, or lack thereof. His temperature, his pulse, his breath rate, his blood pressure—more information than the most concerned citizen could ever want is released several times a day. But it's still difficult to ascertain how much longer Hirohito will be able to hold on.

Humanitarian reasons aside, the Human Rights Now! people are concerned because if the Emperor dies, Japan will go into a period of mourning, and the concert will be cancelled. One wag is moved to suggest that the Concerts for Human Rights Foundation make shirts with the slogan, 'Hang in there, Hirohito', printed on them.

From Amnesty International's point of view, Japan is a crucial stop on the tour. Despite the country's high literacy rate and prosperity, the Japanese people are not major supporters of Amnesty. This section, which was formed 10 years ago, has only 4,000 members, and a recent survey revealed that only about 10 per cent of the population knows the organization's work.

'In Japan, the collective is more important than the individual,' says Sophie Shinozaki, who co-ordinates the section's work with Amnesty's International Secretariat. 'In addition, there's a tendency to think that Amnesty is extreme, that it's political, and people look on it with some suspicion.'

As a result, the section has had to alter its tactics to increase membership and awareness. Instead of emphasizing that Amnesty tries to help individuals who are unjustly imprisoned—a notion that's not particularly appealing to the Japanese—the section now focuses on the fact that ordinary people work on behalf of other ordinary people. The section has also got endorsements from well-known personalities, including poets and artists; and its chairperson is Edith Hanson, an American who moved to Japan several years ago and is now a popular TV actress here. 'People in Japan won't trust an organization that's political unless there are other people in the organization who they can trust,' explains Shinozaki.

Japanese rock fans are also a different breed from their counterparts in Europe and North America. Their fascination with Western culture in general, and rock and roll in particular, is so intense that several times during the two-day visit fans stop Jon Landau, Bruce Springsteen's manager, and ask for his autograph. 'Do you know how often that happens in America?' Landau asks. 'Never.' At the same time, however, the fans apologize profusely for bothering him and act as if they've committed some serious breach of etiquette—which, given traditional Japanese culture, they probably have.

Bruce takes the tube in Tokyo

hat same mixture of aggressiveness and timidity is also apparent at the press conference, which is held on Monday afternoon at the Tokyo Dome, a brand-new indoor baseball stadium with the unlikely nickname of 'The Big Egg'. At first, the reporters seem afraid to ask any questions, and Springsteen, amused by the silence, jokingly asks, 'Does that mean we can go home?' When the journalists finally get up their nerve,

Japanese drumming

'The Big Egg'

conflict with a previously scheduled solo concert in Tokyo.

When the news conference is over, Springsteen returns to the hotel via the tube. Like most of Tokyo, the underground is clean and efficient, a far cry from the mass-transportation systems in New York and London. Though a few people ask for his autograph, most of the riders keep a polite distance, and Springsteen is able to enjoy a few rare moments of peace in a public setting.

Come Tuesday morning, the good news is that the Emperor is still alive, and the concert can go on as scheduled. The show gets under way at three in the afternoon—rock concerts generally start quite early in Japan—and the artists have the rather unfortunate task of performing the opening song 'Get Up, Stand Up' to a half-empty house.

By the time Chapman takes the stage, at about five p.m., roughly 37,000 people have filed into the stadium—a decent crowd, but still 11,000 shy of the Dome's capacity. Because of the Emperor's illness, several public events have already been cancelled as a sign of respect, and it seems likely that under different circumstances, tonight's crowd would have been much larger.

The response to both Chapman's and Gabriel's sets is typically Japanese. The fans sit politely in their seats, applauding after each number but hardly displaying the kind of emotion one normally sees at a rock show in the West. That changes, however, once Springsteen takes the stage. Prior to his performance, the audience is instructed, in both Japanese and English, not to leave their seats, not to stand on their chairs and not to move into the aisles. Surprisingly, the message is to little avail; like fans all around the world, these Japanese teenagers are moved by the sheer power of Springsteen's music, and by his overwhelming stage presence. From start to finish, the fans are on their feet, throwing their fists into the air, and singing along. It's an impressive sight, one that confirms the fact that Springsteen is, quite simply, the most compelling rock performer in the world today.

however, they have some fairly pointed queries, including one about Japan's role as South Africa's main trading partner. 'This tour spells out a vision,' responds Jack Healey. 'And it's quite clear that South Africa does not share that vision.' A few minutes later, Healey adds: 'I should point out that when Japanese people visit South Africa, they are made honorary whites. Perhaps if you're really concerned about the conditions there, you should ask them to make you honorary blacks.' It's a comment that Healey, ever eager to come up with a good line, is quite proud of.

Amnesty's main concern in Japan, however, is the continued existence of the death penalty. Franca Sciuto estimates that 85 people are on death row here and, in its 1988 report, Amnesty states that the organization is seeking 'the commutation of all death sentences' and is urging 'authorities to abolish the death penalty'. But, as Sciuto explains to the reporters, Amnesty's work against the death penalty is complicated by the fact that the Japanese government withholds all information about its death-row population.

Most of the attention at the press conference is focused on Springsteen, probably because, of all the artists on the bill, he has the largest following in Japan. Neither Peter Gabriel nor Tracy Chapman has ever toured here before, and Sting is once again absent, due to a

DELHI

The flight from Tokyo to Delhi lasts only eight hours, but it takes the Human Rights Now! tour from a nation of great wealth and comfort to a nation of poverty, disease and turmoil, a nation whose internal troubles are of great concern to Amnesty International. In its 1988 report, Amnesty outlines several examples of human-rights abuses in India, including the detainment, without charge or trial, of thousands of political activists; unlawful killings by police and paramilitary forces; widespread political violence, particularly in the state of Punjab, where a recent constitutional amendment permits the government to proclaim an emergency and suspend fundamental rights; torture and ill-treatment of political prisoners, who claim to have been beaten, subjected to electrical shocks and otherwise abused; the 'disappearance' of 32 people in Meerut, a city north-east of Delhi; and the on-going enforcement of the death penalty.

In short, Amnesty International has been extremely harsh on the Indian government, and, in turn, Prime Minister Rajiv Gandhi has criticized the organization, saying he doubts its credibility and seriousness. As a result, this concert has been one of the most problematic of the entire tour. And even as the entourage arrives in Delhi on Wednesday night, several matters remain unresolved. For instance, according to Bill Graham, who came to India in advance of the show, the concert's local sponsor, The Times of India, has been advertising the event solely as a celebration of the newspaper's 150th anniversary, with little or no mention of human rights. The Times, however, denies Graham's allegations.

There are other issues, as well, including the price of tickets, some 1,500 of which cost as much as $140 (while others are selling for as little as $3.50), and the role of Amnesty in the pre-concert press conference. By the time the press conference gets under way on Thursday afternoon at the Hyatt Regency Hotel, most of these matters have been dealt with, but there remains a palpable tension in the air. By mutual agreement, Franca Sciuto and local representatives of Amnesty International will not take part in the press conference; however, the artists, keen to publicize Amnesty's involvement in the tour, make it clear in their opening

**Happy Birthday,
Youssou and Babacar!**

Shock the monkey?

Eyeing souvenir postcards

When in Delhi ...

Indian musician Shankar, touring with Gabriel's band, is joined by Springsteen on harmonica for a song written especially for the Delhi concert

remarks that this is an Amnesty International concert, a concert for Human Rights Now! As Bruce Springsteen says, 'We didn't come all this way for a birthday party.'

Likewise, the artists make clear their displeasure over the high-priced tickets. 'We were disgusted when we heard about the ticket prices,' Peter Gabriel says when one reporter points out that many Indians would have to work for six or eight months to earn enough money to afford a ticket. 'And,' adds Gabriel, 'we are not happy about the agreement with *The Times of India*.' That agreement, according to Gabriel, states that although the show may gross as much as $1.2 million, the newspaper is only obliged to give the Concerts Foundation $50,000, with the profits going to non-governmental organizations of the newspaper's choosing. 'We're here for human rights,' says Gabriel, 'and the money raised by this concert should go to Amnesty International. If that's not acceptable, then it should go to another human-rights organization.'

None the less, the artists make a point of stressing how delighted they are to play in India. 'I was here seven years ago,' says Sting, 'and I longed to come back, because I fell in love with India. I fell in love with its splendour and with its contradictions.'

'To visit this country is an important moment for me,' notes Gabriel. 'As a teenager, I was very inspired to read the work of Mahatma Gandhi. Back then, India was giving the whole world an example of non-violent human rights. I hope that in the future this country will again be able to set that kind of example.'

Adds Springsteen: 'Last night, we drove through Old Delhi. As I saw the people sleeping on the streets, I realized things are the

human rights to every person. The pledge "needs a new life force and you can provide it". That's the message Tracy Chapman, Peter Gabriel, Bruce Springsteen, Youssou N'Dour and Sting bring to Delhi.'

Still, relations between the Concerts for Human Rights Foundation and *The Times of India* remain incredibly strained, and throughout the day on Friday both sides threaten to call off the show. Perhaps realizing that a cancellation at such a late date would prove disastrous to all involved, the concert does go on as scheduled, starting at seven p.m. at Nehru Stadium, a surprisingly sleek, modern structure that, like so many in Delhi, stands in stark contrast to the almost unimaginable poverty that surrounds it.

Though the audience seems not to recognize a good portion of the music — Gabriel's 'Sledgehammer' is the first song of the night that draws an immediate and knowing response from the crowd — the 50,000 fans are none the less wildly enthusiastic. And the human-rights message does come across. Early in the evening, hundreds of petitions in support of the Universal Declaration of Human Rights are gathered and turned over to Foundation officials.

Ultimately, though, the show is marred by an incident between photographers and the concert's security people, which results in a shoving match and threats from *The Times of India* that the guards will be turned over to local police. That doesn't happen, but Saturday's papers give the brawl nearly as much coverage as the music, and a second press conference is held, during which Jack Healey attempts to undo the damage done by the bad publicity.

Meanwhile, in one of the hotel restaurants, the atmosphere is far more joyous, as Sting, Gabriel and other musicians help Youssou N'Dour celebrate his 29th birthday. In a way, it's almost a symbolic celebration, because the artists, and the artists alone, through their inspired performances at Nehru Stadium, were responsible for salvaging what could easily have been a disastrous visit.

same here as in my own country, where people are sleeping on the streets of New York and Los Angeles. It's worlds apart, yet it's the same world. We live different lives, but we dream the same dreams and we share the same problems.'

Fuelled by the various controversies, the press conference is easily the most potent of the tour. And while legitimate questions can be raised about the wisdom of performing under such circumstances, the next day's newspapers indicate that, at the very least, the concert will be able to achieve its goal of increasing awareness of human rights. All of the papers devote an enormous amount of space to the tour and its message. Even *The Times of India*, which essentially ignores the debate over its role in the concert, plays up the human-rights angle: 'Time and again governments have violated the historic promise made on 10 December 1948, which guarantees basic

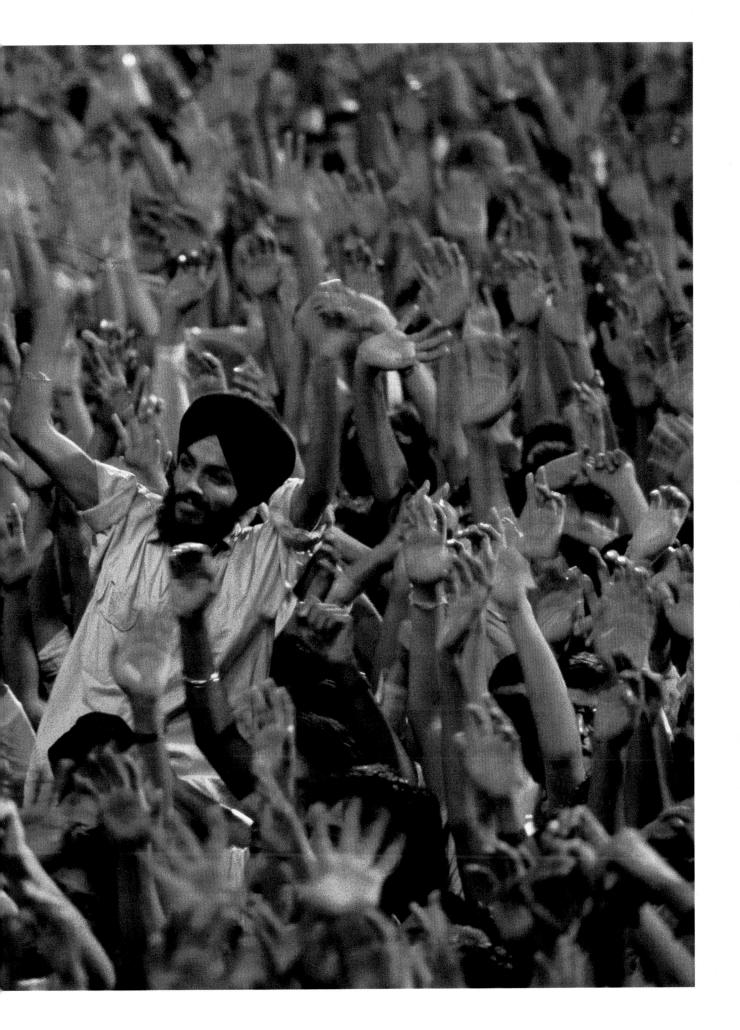

ATHENS

'We don't know where we're going, and we don't know how we're gonna get there,' Bruce Springsteen jokes as the Human Rights Now! DC-10 sits on the tarmac at Indira Gandhi International Airport in Delhi. It's Saturday afternoon, and, unfortunately, Springsteen's comment is close to the truth. A work slow-down by air-traffic controllers in Greece has made it questionable whether the plane will be able to land in Athens. And that's not the only problem. Because Athens was added to the itinerary at the last minute, preparations are way behind schedule. Tickets for the show went on sale just three days ago. And now a football match, set for Sunday afternoon at the same stadium where the concert is to be held, has created seemingly insurmountable production problems. So, as most of the entourage is waiting to leave Delhi, meetings are taking place in Athens to try and reach a compromise whereby construction of the stage can begin on time.

As the tour heads into its final two weeks, the pressure is beginning to wear everyone down. Springsteen and his band, for example, didn't get off-stage in Delhi until half past three in the morning, and the musicians are extremely exhausted. Tracy Chapman has been fighting a cold and severe sore throat for the past several days, and has had to skip the concert's finale in both Tokyo and Delhi. Only Sting, who returned to the line-up in Delhi after a week away from the tour, seems to be operating with his usual amount of energy.

There's also an increasing amount of friction between the various people involved in the tour, which is perhaps inevitable, given the circumstances. No one has ever attempted a tour of this magnitude, with its complicated and demanding logistics, its enormous amount of travel, and its almost total lack of days off. In addition, each party — Amnesty, the artists, the activists, the road crew, Reebok — has its priorities, and at times they can't help but come into conflict. Finally, there's a difference in working styles. Bruce Springsteen's organization, for example, runs a tight-knit, efficient operation that's benefited from years of touring, while some of the people on the tour tend to be more flamboyant, and others

are having to deal with the demands of the road for the first time.

When the flight to Athens finally does take off, the atmosphere inside the plane is abnormally calm, as nearly everyone is using the eight-hour flight as a chance to catch up on some much-needed sleep. There are, of course, a few exceptions. Up in the front cabin, Clarence Clemons has organized a poker game, and he occasionally gets on the plane's PA system to try and entice other members of the entourage to join in. And Max Loubiere, one of Springsteen's aides, is handing out ballots for this week's American football pool, the winner of which can pocket as much as $800. And then there are the in-flight movies. The selections are inexplicably limited, and for the third time on the tour, *Caddyshack* is showing up on the screens, followed by *Good Morning, Vietnam*, which is making its second appearance of the tour.

The flight manages to touch down in Athens on time, but the labour problems delay the delivery of the entourage's luggage until the wee hours of the morning, resulting in yet another late night for everyone. On Sunday, several people take in the sights, visiting the Acropolis and other historic monuments around the city. At four o'clock, the usual pre-concert press conference is held, but with

a slightly more dramatic twist. Freedom House, located in a park not far from one of the entourage's hotels, used to be a torture centre during the seven years when Greece was ruled by a dictatorship. Pericles Pangalos, the head of Amnesty's Greek section, was one of the people who endured the wrath of the military junta there, and Sunday marks the first time he's returned since his release more than a decade ago. He welcomes the artists to Greece, noting that it is the country where democracy was born and a country where, on several occasions, 'democracy has been wounded'. And he points out the victory that is implicit in the fact that a human-rights press conference can now be held in a place where horrible abuses once occurred.

Back at the hotel, the tour's organizers are still trying to sort out the problems that threaten the Athens show. After several meetings, they finally work out an arrangement under which the construction of the stage can begin, enabling the concert to go on as planned. Meanwhile, tickets are selling so rapidly that Bill Graham brings up the possibility of a second show here; not surprisingly, the suggestion meets with resistance from the other organizers who, at this point, are reluctant to add any dates to the schedule. There is, however, one exception: the Soviet Union. The artists still haven't given up hope of a show there, and on Monday they plan to send another message to General Secretary Mikhail Gorbachev, seeking approval for a concert. 'We feel it's very important that this tour stop in the Soviet Union,' Jack Healey says at the press conference. 'And we will continue to ask the Soviet leaders to allow us to come to their country.'

On Sunday night, several of the artists head to a traditional Greek restaurant to celebrate Sting's 37th birthday. By the end of the evening, almost everyone has let their hair down: one belly-dancer tries to unbutton Springsteen's shirt, Sting then volunteers to take off his own shirt, and even Peter Gabriel gets into the act, with an impressive display of traditional Greek dancing.

The biggest excitement of the day, however, comes when Veronica De-Negri, one of the human-rights activists on the tour, receives news that the Inter-American Human Rights Commission of the Organization of American States has issued an order that lays responsibility for the death of her son, Rodrigo Rojas, on the Chilean government. The order states that the government violated, among other things, Article 1 of the Universal Declaration of Human Rights when its military police set Rodrigo on fire and left him to die. It asks that reparations be paid to his family, and to Carmen Quintana, who was badly burned in the incident, and that the government make an effort to bring the responsible parties to trial. Needless to say, several toasts are made in Veronica's honour when the Amnesty people get together for a Sunday-night dinner.

Olympic Stadium is nearly filled to its 70,000 capacity when the Athens show gets under way on Monday afternoon. The crowd is one of the more animated of the tour, and fans hold candles aloft during both Tracy Chapman's and Peter Gabriel's sets. Sting also turns in a vibrant performance, adding two old Police songs, 'Driven to Tears' and 'Roxanne' to his set. Backstage, however, there is much squabbling among the various camps, and it seems that the majority of the entourage is looking forward to arriving in Harare, Zimbabwe, the tour's next stop, where two free days miraculously have been slipped into the schedule.

HARARE

122

This is the front line. Here in Zimbabwe, the human-rights message cuts far deeper than in almost any other place the Human Rights Now! tour has visited. Zimbabwe gained its independence only eight years ago, and its policy of reconciliation between blacks and whites stands as an example for the rest of Southern Africa. And, because of its proximity to the Republic of South Africa — and the fact that as many as 20,000 South Africans have come north to see this show — this is one concert at which the artists have a chance to drive their point home clearly and directly. As Bruce Springsteen says, when asked what effect he hopes the event will have on the visiting South Africans, 'I hope they will go home and lend their hearts and voices to the struggle for freedom in their own country.'

The entourage arrives in Harare on Tuesday night. It's springtime here, and the jacaranda trees are in full, brilliant bloom, the temperature is in the 80s, and the sky is clear and blue. For those visiting Africa for the first time, Harare comes as something of a shock, for it resembles nothing so much as a medium-sized city in the midwestern part of the United States, circa 1960. The streets are wide, well-paved and clean; the buildings in the city centre are low, fairly modern and clean. In other words, the city is a far cry from the average westerner's preconceptions of the Third World. It's not exotic or strange; it's not that different from the places where many of these musicians grew up.

Wednesday is a day off, one of the only days of the tour when absolutely nothing is scheduled: no press conference, no concert, no travel. About 100 members of the entourage, including Springsteen, Sting and Tracy Chapman, take advantage of this rare leisure time and travel to Victoria Falls, one of the seven natural wonders of the world. There, the artists can walk around virtually unrecognized by both the tourists and the locals. It's truly relaxing, it's truly a magnificent sight, and it goes a long way toward easing the friction that many have felt over the past several days.

Thursday is press-conference day and, predictably, most of the questions focus on South Africa. When one reporter asks, in a rather derogatory tone, if the musicians have anything specific to say about the situation there, Springsteen holds up a copy of the Universal Declaration of Human Rights and proceeds to read several articles that the South African government, by virtue of its policy of apartheid, clearly violates. He then concludes by saying, 'They have a lot of work to do.'

As the artists go on to discuss the cultural boycott of South Africa, and the possibility that the show's PA system may have come indirectly from that country, the press conference once again demonstrates the commitment that these musicians have to the tour and to the cause of human rights. Over the course of the last five weeks, the artists — particularly Springsteen and Chapman — have become far more comfortable and self-confident in this setting, and these gatherings have turned into lively, provocative and entertaining forums.

But, of course, the real power of the tour emanates from the music, and Friday night's show is easily one of the best. Everything seems to be working: the energy level is high, the chemistry between the

Sightseeing at Victoria Falls

Crew member 'Chainsaw' wants you to get the message!

123

artists is apparent from the stage and, most important of all, there's an even greater-than-usual sense of purpose. Spurred on by the special political and social circumstances of the show, the musicians turn in powerful, passionate performances. The crowd, about 72,000 strong, is racially mixed — about 60 per cent white, in fact — and that seems to enhance the feelings that this concert presents a rare opportunity to reach those who can help change the situation in South Africa, a point Peter Gabriel emphasizes when he introduces 'Biko'.

tour, and Gabriel is barely able to contain himself.

Tracy Chapman's set follows, and she receives a loud, boisterous welcome. Her album is near the top of the charts here and in South Africa, and in many way she seems to be the artist most eagerly anticipated. Like Gabriel, she doesn't mince any words in expressing her anger over the situation in South Africa. 'This concert tonight is for everyone,' she says before performing 'Freedom Now'. 'In some ways, it's more for those people who can't be here, because they couldn't afford the tickets, or because they are in jail. This concert is most of all for those people, and we must tell the Bothas and Pinochets of the world that we will not stand by while people are tortured, while people are homeless, while people have no jobs.'

Peter Gabriel and Youssou N'Dour sing 'In Your Eyes'

'This song was written ten years ago for a very brave man,' he says. 'I'm very proud to be able to sing it so close to the source.' He then refers to the reports that part of the sound system may have come from South Africa. 'If that's true,' he says, 'then I want to sing even louder so that this song is heard all through South Africa.' And, indeed, it is. Thanks to a live radio hook-up with Capital Radio, Gabriel's stunning tribute to the slain African activist is fed directly over the airwaves in South Africa. It's a moving, emotional performance, one of the most dramatic of the

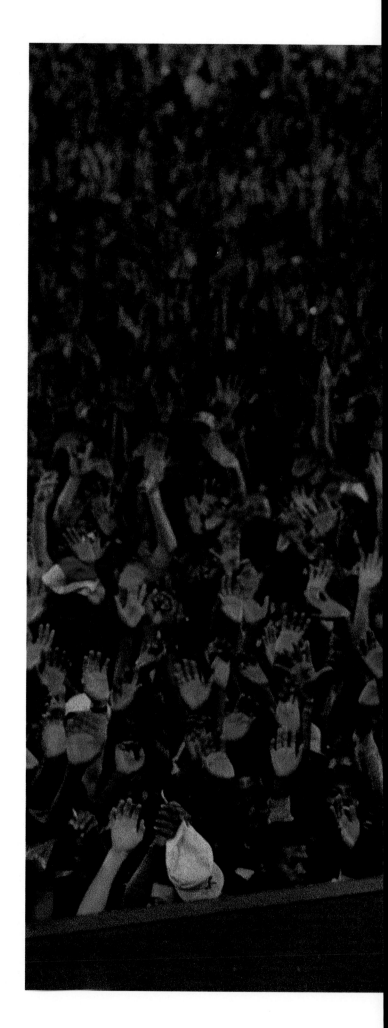

In the end, however, it's Bruce Springsteen who blasts the message of the Universal Declaration of Human Rights back to Johannesburg with all the force of a fire-and-brimstone preacher. Diverting from his usual stage rap about the relationship between rock and roll and freedom, Springsteen instead uses the occasion to construct a long, articulate plea for change, both in South Africa and in the United States. It's a stunning oration that draws parallels between the young American men who were drafted to fight the Vietnam War and the young South African men who currently face mandatory conscription. And it ties together the horrors of apartheid in South Africa and the horrors of the economic and racial inequality that still exist in the United States. His message to the audience — and to those in South Africa who are hearing Springsteen over Capital Radio — is clear: take charge of your life, be informed about what's going on in the world. It's up to you to make the world a better place.

The next day, Springsteen calls the performance one of the two or three greatest shows of his entire career. and there's little doubt that he's absolutely right.

HARARE

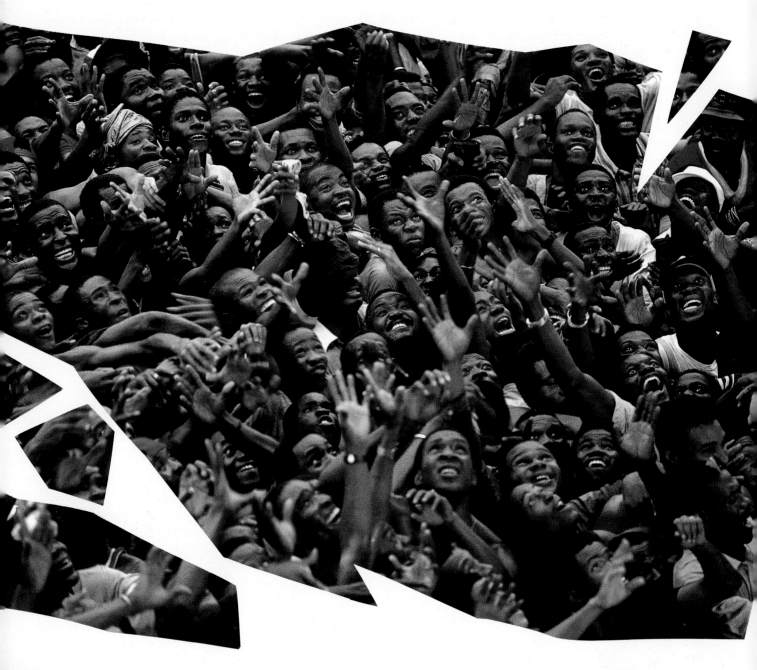

ABIDJAN

128

BRUCE SPRINGSTEEN
& THE E-STREET BAND
JOHNNY CLEGG AND SAVUKA
PETER GABRIEL
STING
TRACY CHAPMAN
YOUSSOU N'DOUR

DIMANCHE 9 OCTOBRE 1988/16 H
STADE HOUPHOUET-BOIGNY · ABIDJAN

N° 24952

DIMANCHE 9 OCT. 1988 / 16 H
STADE HOUPHOUET-BOIGNY
ABIDJAN

2000 Francs CFA

N° 24952

As the Human Rights Now! caravan moves to Western Africa, the musicians are still fired up by their experience in Harare. All of them agree that the show there was remarkable, one they'll never forget. At the press conference in Abidjan on Saturday, Bruce Springsteen stresses the importance of the event. 'Unfortunately,' he says, 'most of the audiences I draw in the US are white. In Harare, I had the first chance to play to an integrated audience. There's a point where I ask everyone to raise their hands. Looking out into the audience and seeing black hands raised with white hands was a very emotional moment for me. For when black hands are raised with white hands, when rich hands are raised with poor hands, that is when governments tremble. And that is when they will pay more attention to this document, the Universal Declaration of Human Rights.'

Earlier in the press conference, Springsteen talked about Amnesty International's 1988 Report, a detailed, country-by-country analysis of human-rights abuses around the world. The 1988 edition, which was published a few days ago, paints what Amnesty calls an 'ugly picture' of world-wide human-rights violations. It includes the following revelations:

- In at least half of the countries of the world, people are locked away for speaking their minds, 'often after trials that are no more than a sham'.
- In more than a third of the nations, men, women and even children are tortured by government officials.
- In scores of countries, governments pursue their goals by kidnapping and murdering their own citizens.
- More than 120 states have written into their laws the right to execute people convicted of certain crimes, and more than a third carry out such premeditated killings every year.

In addition, the report states that, during 1987, prisoners of conscience were held in at least 80 countries, torture or ill-treatment of prisoners took place in at least 90 countries,

and more than 760 prisoners were executed in 39 countries.

Despite such facts, the report offers a glimmer of hope, noting that there now exists a genuinely world-wide human-rights movement made up of more than a thousand organizations. 'Today, even one death can set off waves of anger and protest,' the report says. 'The torture and death in 1987 of one student in South Korea—Park Chong-chol—led to publicity, followed by the arrest of police officers and the resignation of government ministers. It doesn't always happen, but it can.'

Overall, however, the press conference is less exhilarating than usual, and much of the reporters' attention focuses on the fact that, instead of a legitimately local act, the promoters in Abidjan have added Johnny Clegg to the bill. Clegg, the former leader of the band Juluka and a major star in Western Africa, is a white South African who has been an outspoken critic of his

Johnny Clegg and band

country's government and its policies. 'I sit here tonight with a very heavy feeling in my heart,' Clegg says. 'For I come from a country that has systematically eliminated many of the rights in this book.' He holds up a copy of the Universal Declaration. 'That country is South Africa.'

Clegg goes on to cite specific examples of the abuses that have taken place in South Africa over the past few years. He then concludes by saying, 'For me, it is a responsibility and a duty to participate in this particular show. We have to look at the twentieth century as a whole. It has seen some of the worst and some of the best developments in history. There are only 12 years left before the end of the century, and one gets a sense from young people that the world is coming together. Young people are eager for a new order. This concert, and this entire tour, is an attempt to regain the proper image of man and to regain the respect for man's rights and dignity.'

One of the reasons Clegg was added to the bill was to bolster ticket sales. Advance sales had been slow, and, even as late as Sunday morning, there was some concern that the artists would be playing to a nearly empty house. But when they arrive for the four o'clock opening, the field is packed. Thousands of young black Ivorians

are here, and they're obviously ready to have a good time.

The line-up has been juggled, in part so that Youssou N'Dour, who lives in nearby Senegal, can take the stage later than usual. As a result, Sting goes on first, and the audience, which is crammed up to the edge of the stage, literally erupts, their bodies swaying back and forth, their arms raised in the air. The reception energizes Sting, and he delivers one of his strongest performances of the tour.

Meanwhile, outside the stadium, a stand-off has developed between local police and a group of Ivorian military men, who feel they deserve free entry into the concert. Both sides

Held aloft by an ecstatic crowd

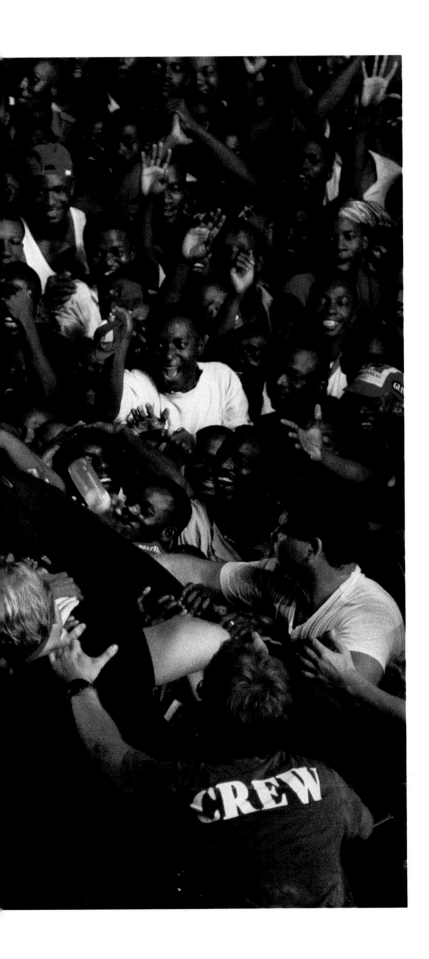

Gabriel takes the plunge . . .

. . . and emerges, minus his shirt

are armed, and it takes a good hour before the *brouhaha* finally subsides and the soldiers give up. Similar incidents have occurred elsewhere along the way, and they serve as a potent reminder of just how far this tour has strayed outside the normal boundaries of rock and roll.

Back inside, it seems little could dampen the spirits of the crowd. The mostly male fans greet Tracy Chapman with chants of 'Tray-cee, Tray-cee', and a few of them even throw her kisses. The high point of the show, however, comes during Peter Gabriel's set, when, at the end of 'Lay Your Hands on Me', he falls backward into the crowd. He loses his shirt in the process, but emerges unscathed. It's a fantastic testament to his enormous faith, both in mankind and in the power of rock and roll.

Springsteen's set is equally explosive and well-recieved, and, in the van on the way back to the hotel, the artists take an impromptu vote. The Abidjan show, they all agree, was the best yet.

133

SÃO PAULO

With this show, the Human Rights Now! tour has come full circle. Ten months ago, here in São Paulo, the tour was officially announced. Now, after the amazingly successful concerts in Africa, the entourage has arrived in South America for the final three shows.

There's a sense of both relief and sadness. After six weeks on the road, a lot of people are eager to get back home, to their families, their jobs, a more familiar and stable environment. Yet, at the same time, there's a type of bonding that occurs when so many people are travelling together for such a long period of time and under such unusual circumstances. And, on this tour, those bonds have been strengthened by the fact that almost everyone is working toward a goal that's far greater than on a normal rock-and-roll tour.

And, despite the many problems the tour has encountered along the way — the last-minute schedule changes, the personality clashes, the general sense of chaos — there seems to be agreement that it has all been worthwhile, that it has accomplished its goals. With few exceptions, the visits to each city have expanded awareness of human rights. Local media have devoted much space to the fact that this is more than a rock-and-roll tour, and Amnesty sections have benefited from the massive exposure. In Greece, for example,

more than 2,500 people contacted Amnesty in the days after the concert, wanting to know how to join. And the tiny Amnesty groups in both Japan and India received far more publicity in a matter of days than had been possible in the entire history of their existence.

In a large part, the responsibility for the tour's success must go to the artists. Throughout the six-week tour, they have stayed above the fray, setting an example of co-operation and commitment even as things were on the verge of exploding behind the scenes. In city after city, their appearances at the press conferences continually improved. And on-stage each night, they not only delivered some of the best performances of their careers, but they also addressed the subject of human rights in such a way that Amnesty was able to deliver its message to hundreds of thousands of people who otherwise may never have heard of the organization.

And so, as the tour winds down, the feelings are mixed, but the energy level remains high. When the DC-10 touches down in São Paulo, hundreds of fans are waiting for a glimpse of the artists. Here in South America, it's Sting who garners the greatest amount of attention. He's toured here before, both with the Police and on his own, and, as he says at the press conference on

Prominent Brazilian singer, Milton Nascimento

135

Indian chief of the Kaiapo
tribe, Raoni, applies war-
paint to Sting's face

Tuesday afternoon, he's developed a particular
fondness for Brazil. He's also deeply troubled
by many of the issues facing the country.

'Brazil is a land of many problems, poverty,
hunger, inflation and the destruction of its
environment,' he says. 'Each year, developing
nations pay $30 billion in interest to the rich
banks in the North. I don't want to live in a
world where half the people are starving and
the other half are fat and rich.'

But the issue most bothersome to Sting is
the mistreatment of the country's native Indians and the related destruction of the rain
forest by cattle ranchers, loggers, gold miners
and other entrepreneurs. 'It was once a kind of
science-fiction idea that the planet would be in
danger,' he says. 'But now it's actually come to
pass in our own lifetime. It's a scientific given
that if the rain forest goes, then the climate will
flip-flop and the Amazon will become another
Sahara. Frankly, I would rather have a rain
forest than another lousy hamburger.'

The severity of the problem became apparent to him last year, when, during a break
from his South American tour, he and a
Belgian film-maker named Jean-Pierre Dubil-
leux made an excursion into the rain forest to
visit the Kaiapo Indians. 'We spent about four
hours in a plane, flying over what looked like a
desert,' Sting says. 'It was red, dusty, a few tree

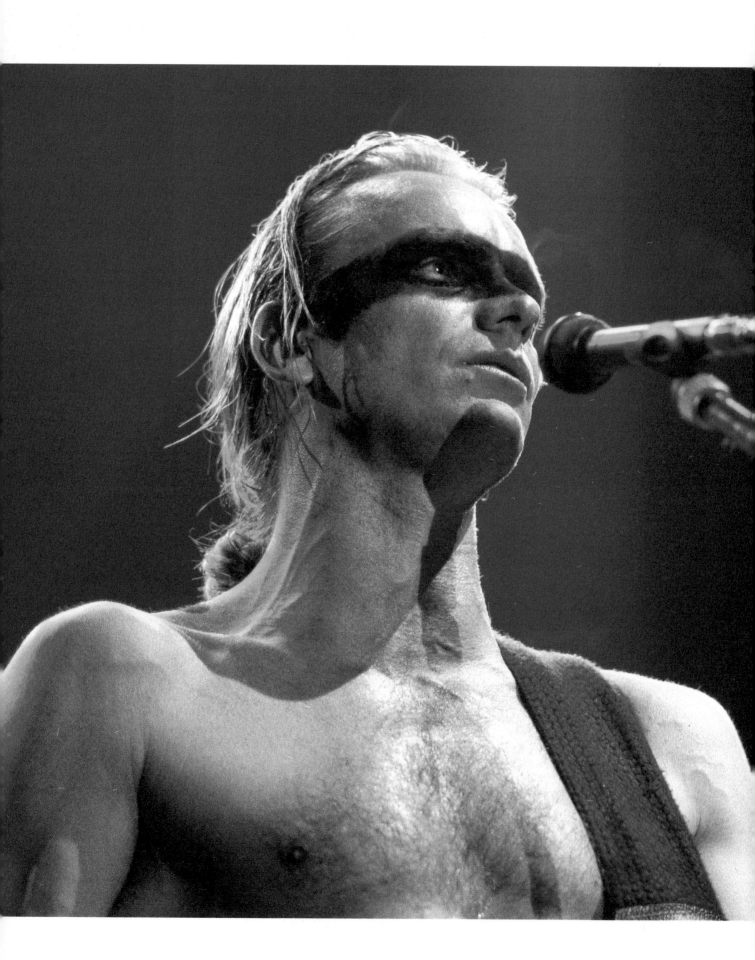

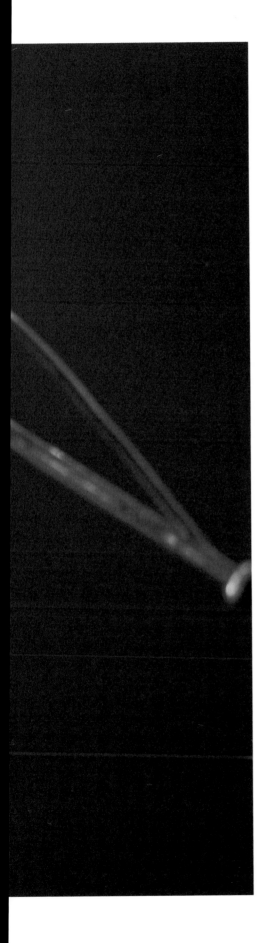

stumps. My friend, Jean-Pierre, looked sad and I asked him what was wrong. And he said, "Well, when I first came here 15 years ago, this was all forest."'

During the visit, Sting befriended some members of the Kaiapo tribe and its chief, Raoni. And so, during the press conference, he sets aside his usual text and instead makes an impassioned plea for the protection of the rain forest and the dwindling Indian population, which now numbers only 200,000.

His comments actually bring some results. On Wednesday morning, the Brazilian government issues a statement saying that it's trying to do something about the problem and is considering enacting some policy reforms. Still, Sting isn't convinced that the changes will be anything more than cosmetic, and, urged on by the Kaiapo, makes plans for a symbolic journey around a section of the rain forest, which they want the government to protect and preserve.

On Wednesday night, Sting again presses the issue, this time from the stage. Raoni then joins him onstage, and applies war-paint to Sting's face. They then sing a traditional Indian song, 'Tama Tama Teo Ay', about coming home. 'I am here because our land is being invaded by prospectors and farmers,' Raoni says. 'I want Brazil to respect the Indians, and the government of Brazil to protect our land.'

139

MENDOZA

Tour Director Bill Graham

The previous night's press conference

I f you look over the top of the stage at Estadio Mundialista, a small, modern football stadium, you can glimpse the peaks of the Andes. It's a breathtaking view, as pretty as you'll see from just about any sports stadium in the world. But, here in Mendoza, the Andes are more than just a beautiful mountain range. They are a dividing line, a natural boundary that separates Argentina, a country that is still in the process of healing the wounds suffered during seven years of dictatorship, and Chile, a country where, over the past 15 years, some of the most brutal human-rights abuses in recent history have taken place under the iron fist of General Augusto Pinochet.

On 5 October, just nine days before the Human Rights Now! tour arrives in Mendoza, the citizens of Chile said no to Pinochet in a plebiscite held to determine whether he would stay in power until 1997. And so, as Chilean poet Ariel Dorfman says, 'This is a celebration. This is a concert for Chile. If Pinochet had won the plebiscite, it would have been a protest. But we said no, and it's a celebration.'

Some 15,000 Chileans have travelled across the border to take part in this celebration. On Thursday night, they took to the streets of Mendoza, turning it into a Chilean city and raising their voices in a joyous expression of freedom. 'When you've been oppressed for so long,' says Dorfman, 'and suddenly you have the opportunity to go out and say what you want and not have to worry about being arrested, it has a great effect on the human spirit.'

It was Dorfman who, several months ago, suggested to Jack Healey that the Human

Rehearsal with Inti Illimani, exiled Chilean folk group

Sting meets with Ariel Dorfman, Chilean poet, and Carmen Quintana, burn victim

Rights Now! tour stop in Mendoza. 'Mendoza is the nearest frontier city,' explains Dorfman, a long-time Amnesty ally. 'For years, Chileans have used the city as a place where they can come across the border and meet with exiles who were not permitted to come into their own country.'

But equally important to Dorfman was the symbolic value a show in Mendoza would have. 'The artists would be singing from a country that had terrible human-rights violations to a country where abuses are still occurring. It would be a peaceful army of voices crossing the Andes.'

At around the same time Dorfman contacted Healey, the members of the exiled Chilean folk group Inti Illimani — who are among the three local acts on the bill here — suggested the same idea to Sting and Peter Gabriel. 'I think it was significant that a Chilean writer and a Chilean musical group both wanted to play in Mendoza,' Dorfman says. 'I think that's the reason the concert happened.'

There were, however, other factors that made the concert here inevitable. Veronica De-Negri, one of the activists accompanying the Human Rights Now! tour, is an exiled Chilean whose son, Rodrigo Rojas, was killed by Chilean security police in an incident that attracted attention throughout the world. For Veronica, this is a sort of home-coming, and, at the press conference in Buenos Aires on Thursday night, Healey dedicates the show to De-Negri and her two sons, Rodrigo and Pablo (who is also taking part in the tour).

In addition, Sting's song 'They Dance Alone' has become something of an anthem among those fighting oppression in Chile and, in fact, played a fairly prominent role in the campaign to defeat Pinochet. 'Every city I've played in on my current tours, I've met los Chileans,' Sting says. 'And each one of them has said the same thing to me: thanks for writing the song, thanks for remembering what happened, thanks for telling the world what still happens in Chile. And I'm so happy that the Chilean people have had the strength to say no to a man like Pinochet.'

The Chileans' gratitude to Sting is expressed early on in Mendoza, where a group of women — members of the Association of Missing and Detained Persons of Chile — come backstage to greet him. The women are the mothers, the sisters, the daughters of men who have 'disappeared' under the Pinochet regime. Their heads are covered with white scarves, and around their necks they wear pictures of their loved ones, inscribed with the words '¿Donde Estan?' While three of the women play guitars, and others sing, one woman does the dance that Sting so eloquently describes in 'They Dance Alone'. It's an emotional scene and a powerful expression of just how meaningful the song has been to the people of Chile.

Also backstage is Carmen Quintana, the young woman who was accompanying Rodrigo Rojas when he was burned to death. She is still badly scarred from the attack, and much of her body is covered in bandages. 'I am only 21 years old,' she says. 'And I am a living testimony of what torture is in my country. But I am also a testimony of the fact that hope continues. And I know that one day my country will again be free.'

In terms of sheer enthusiasm, no other audience on this tour has been as ecstatic or demonstrative as the one here tonight. But what makes this a truly special concert is the presence of people like Quintana, De-Negri and the relatives of the 'disappeared'. They are the people that this tour is about, the people for whom the artists, the activists and the crew members have been working so long and so hard.

MENDOZA

That point is driven home at the end of Sting's set, when he invites about 25 relatives of the 'disappeared' to join him on stage during 'They Dance Alone'. It is, without question, the emotional high point of the entire tour, and it's witnessed by dozens of members of the entourage, who pack the sides of the stage. Afterwards, everyone, from the toughest security men to the most hardened managers, is overwhelmed. Throughout the tour, there had been many people who doubted its wisdom, who questioned its true motives. But after this one ten-minute performance, all of those doubts have been removed, all of those questions have been answered. For this show alone, the Human Rights Now! tour has been worth it all.

Sting and Veronica De-Negri

MENDOZA

BUENOS AIRES

After six weeks on the road, the Human Rights Now! tour has reached its end. This is the final show, and it seems an appropriate time for the artists to have the final word.

Youssou N'Dour 'I honestly feel that we've done something very important, and I'd like to continue to play all over the world and continue spreading the message of Amnesty International. A lot of the people we played for had never had direct contact with the issue of human rights, especially in places like India and Abidjan. When I see places where people are so poor, it touches me. And the people in those places will always remember this moment, the moment the singers came to speak to them about human rights. And I believe that in the future, they will make human rights part of their lives.

'But for me, the best part of the tour was the press conferences. I had never done a press conference before. And after six weeks of being able to express myself, I feel very involved with the issue of human rights. I have a big parcel of papers in my luggage with all my notes and all of the information about each of the countries where we played. Musicians from Africa very rarely have the kind of opportunity that I have had. It was very important for me to go to the different continents and see the different cultures and different peoples. And I know that when I go back to Africa, I will continue to be involved in this issue of human rights.'

Sting 'I was in this from the beginning, so I'm more than pleased that we've actually done it. That we've actually gotten around the world, that we've actually played these concerts. Amnesty has more members. We've had a good time. I can't see any part of the tour that hasn't been a success.

'I think you'd have to be blind, deaf and dumb not to know that this was more than just an entertainment. I'm not sure what percentage of the people who came to see us will go away with a seed planted inside them. I don't know how long that seed will take to flower. But I believe very strongly that in 10 or 15 years, when these young people who came to our concerts inherit the political and social infrastructures of their respective countries, the seed that's been planted about human rights will come to fruition.'

Peter Gabriel 'From the start, the idea of this tour sounded very inspiring to me, because I assumed that most other people in the world knew as little as I did about the Universal Declaration of Human Rights, about its contents and, particularly, about the fact that their governments had agreed to its guarantees on their behalf. So the idea of taking this information around the world seemed very powerful, and I think that we have succeeded in getting that information out.

'And I think that information can be very powerful. For me, this tour has been an education. Not only have I learned a lot more

Sting with Argentinian children of the 'disappeared'

about what's going on in the world, but I also have the feeling that I can influence things. And that's the exciting sense of power that I think a lot of people around this tour, and a lot of people around Amnesty, get to learn. And I think it's important that people who have suffered, who are suffering, and who feel oppression are also aware of that power. If they know that their governments have agreed to the Universal Declaration, then they can fight with that document on their side.

'Amnesty International is a beacon of hope. It's proof that ordinary people have the power to bring about changes. And we have a responsibility to use that power to make the world a better place for our children.'

Tracy Chapman 'This tour has unfortunately only confirmed what I had always thought, that universally people struggle and suffer and are in need of basic essentials and often live in daily fear for their lives.

'But I've also seen a universal desire for change, a desire for a better world. I have faith in people, if only because in believing otherwise, there is no hope. We can change ourselves. Individuals have the potential to be compassionate. We can change the policies of our governments. Together we may one day change the world. If put into practice by all the governments of the world, the Universal

Sting with band members Dolette McDonald, Tracy Wormworth, Branford Marsalis and Mino Cinelu

Declaration of Human Rights would allow for all people to know the true sense of the word freedom. And we as individuals will never be free until all people are free.'

Bruce Springsteen 'This tour was about trying to assert myself as a world citizen. When you grow up in the States, you grow up pretty isolated. And one of the things that is most necessary for American young people is a sense of world consciousness, a sense of the value of all other cultures.

'As a boy, all I knew of Africa and India and South America was what I studied in geography class. And I was not a very good student. But, during this tour, I have become a better student and, I hope, a better man. As we played in Zimbabwe, so close to the apartheid in South Africa, I thought of the economic apartheid that separates the under class in the ghettos of every major city in the United States. As we drove through Old Delhi in India, I saw the poor and homeless sleeping on the streets, and I realized that the homeless

also sleep on the streets in New York and Los Angeles. In Brazil, where, because of land disputes, peasants and human-rights activists are threatened and killed for standing up for justice, I was reminded of the civil-rights struggle in the States during the sixties, when those who stood up for change were harassed and sometimes killed, without intervention by local authorities. And, in Argentina, where the difference between the wealthy and poor is so great, I think of the 15 per cent living below the poverty line in my own home, one of the wealthiest countries in the world.

'The end of this tour marks my graduation of sorts. And I hope that I will be able to go back home and, in my music, write about a different sensibility that I felt on this tour. And I hope to get American young people out of their shells, and into the idea that what happens in Africa, or Asia, or South America is important to them. I would hope to go back and be a voice of sanity and vision that the young people of my country could understand.'

Jack Healey, Sting, Peter, and Youssou all get into the act with Bruce and the E Street Band

The Three Bruces?

154

**Youssou and Sting join
Bruce in the water ritual**

AMNESTY ADDRESSES AROUND THE WORLD

Amnesty Addresses Around the World

There are now more than 3,860 local Amnesty International groups in over 60 countries around the world. In 47 countries these are co-ordinated by sections, whose addresses are given below:

AUSTRALIA
Amnesty International
Australian Section
P.O. Box No. A159
Sydney South
New South Wales 2000

Tel: +61 2 267 2075
Fax: +61 2 261 5018
Telex: 23206 AIAUST AA

New South Wales
Amnesty International
New South Wales Branch
P.O. Box A611
Sydney South
New South Wales 2000

Tel: +61 2 267 9199
Fax: +61 2 261 5018
Telex: 23206 AIAUST AA
    ATT NSW BRANCH

Queensland
Amnesty International
Queensland Branch
Dunstan House,
236 Elizabeth Street
AWU Bldg, 6th floor
Brisbane
Queensland 4000

Tel: +61 7 221 0221
Fax: +61 7 221 4460

South Australia
Amnesty International
South Australia Branch
1st floor, 155 Pirie Street
Adelaide
South Australia 5000

Tel: +61 8 232 0066
Telex: 88420 SACLIB
    (ATT ROB EIME,
    AI SOUTH AUSTRALIA)

Tasmania
Amnesty International
Tasmania Branch
Box No. 968 K GPO
Hobart, Tasmania

Tel: +61 02 34 7858
Telex: 57073 PIJEN (ATT AMNESTY)

Victoria
Amnesty International
Victoria Branch
4 Chatham Street
Prahran. Victoria 3181

Tel: +61 3 51 1972
Telex: 30625 AA ATT ME 3705

Western Australia
Amnesty International
Western Australia Branch
Box X2258, GPO Perth
Western Australia 6001

Tel: +61 9 328 3332
Telex: 94114 MTHL AA

AUSTRIA
Amnesty International
Austrian Section
Wiedner Guertel 12/7
A-1040 Wien

Tel: +43 222 505 4320
Telex: 131704

BANGLADESH
Please send *all* correspondence via the IS, Campaign and Membership Department

BARBADOS
Amnesty International
Barbados Section
P.O. Box 872
Bridgetown
BARBADOS, West Indies

Tel: +1 809 428 9331

BELGIUM
Flemish Branch
Amnesty International
Kerkstraat 156
2008 Antwerpen

Tel: +32 3 271 1616
Telex: 32079

French-Speaking Branch
Amnesty International
9 rue Berckmans
1060 Bruxelles
Tel: +32 2 538 8175-77
Telex: 20237 AMNINT B

BRAZIL
Anistia Internacional
Rua Harmonia 899
05435 – São Paulo – SP

Tel: +55 11 813 5799
    or   8153565
Telex: 1183207 SBAI BR

CANADA
English-Speaking Branch
Canadian Section (English Speaking)
130 Slater Street, Suite 900
Ottawa
Ontario, K1P 6E2

Fax: +1 613 233 6643
Telex: 533295 AMNSTY OTT
Cable: AMSTYCANAD

French-Speaking Branch
Amnistie Internationale
Section Canadienne (francophone)
3516 ave du Parc
Montreal, Quebec
H2X 2H7

Tel: +1 514 288 1141
Fax: +1 514 288 7314
Telex: 5560543 AMSTCANAD
    MTL

CHILE
Señores
Casilla 4062
Santiago

Tel: +5 62 335 897
Telex: 340260 PBVTR CK att AI
    CHILE

COTE D'IVOIRE
Amnesty International
Section Côte d'Ivoire
04 BP 895
Abidjan 04

Tel: +225 324 660

DENMARK
Amnesty International
Danish Section
Frederiksborggade 1
1360 Copenhagen K

Tel: +45 1 11 75 41
Fax: +45 1 93 37 46
Telex: 19641 AMNSTY DK

ECUADOR
Señores
Avenida 10 de agosto, 645, Piso 8
Edificio UCICA, Oficina 806
Quito

Tel: +593 2 527471
Telex: IETEL Hotel Colon 2-2316
    fono 237-495/543-151 IETEL
    ED

FAROE ISLANDS
Amnesty International
Faroe Islands Section
P.O. Box 1075
FR-110 Torshavn

Tel: +298 15816
Telex: 81363 jus FA

FINLAND
Amnesty International
Finnish Section
Ruoholahdenkatu 24
SF – 00180 Helsinki

Tel: +358 0 6931 488
Telex: 123897 AMNES SF

FRANCE
Amnesty International
French Section
4, rue de la Pierre Levee
75553 Paris (Cedex 11)

Tel: +33 1 43 38 74 74
Fax: +33 1 43 38 26 15
Telex: 213659 AMNESTY F

FEDERAL REPUBLIC OF GERMANY
Amnesty International
Section of the FRG
Heerstrasse 178
5300 Bonn 1

Tel: +49 228 650981-3
Fax: +49 228 630036
Telex: 886539 AIBN D

GHANA
Amnesty International
Ghanaian Section
P.O. Box 1173
Koforidua

GREECE
Amnesty International
Greek Section
20 Mavromihali Street
Athens 106–80

Tel: +30 1 360 0628
Telex: 224295 GSAI GR

GUYANA
AI Guyana Section
Palm Court Building
35 Main Street
Georgetown
GUYANA West Indies

HONG KONG
Amnesty International
Hong Kong Section
216 Beverley Commercial Centre
87–105 Chatham Road
Kowloon

Tel: +852 3 7221 872
Fax: +852 3 3114 513

ICELAND
Amnesty International
Icelandic Section
P.O. Box 618
121 Reykjavik

Tel: +354 1 16940

INDIA
Amnesty International
c/o Dateline Delhi
21 North End Complex
Panchkuin Road
New Delhi 110001

Tel: +91 11 310799

IRELAND
Amnesty International
Irish Section
8 Shaw Street
Dublin 2

Tel: +353 1 776361
    0001 776361 (from UK **only**)
Telex: 90428 AIEI

ISRAEL
Amnesty International
Israel Section
P.O. Box 23003
Tel Aviv 61230

Tel: +972 3 286 601
Telex: 361595-6 DANET AL
ATT AMNIL

ITALY
Amnesty International
Italian Section
viale Mazzini 146
00195 Rome

Tel: +39 6 380 898 /389 403
Telex: 620026 AMNEST I

JAPAN
Amnesty International
Japanese Section
Daisan-Sanbu Building 3F
2−3−22 Nishi-Waseda
Shinjuku-ku. Tokyo 160

Tel: +81 3 203 1050
Fax: +81 3 232 6775
Telex: 27890 CCRAI J
ATT AMNESTY

LUXEMBOURG
Amnesty International Luxembourg
Boîte Postale 1914
1019 Luxembourg

Tel: +352 48 16 87
Telex: 3548 AIVIV LU

MEXICO
Seccion Mexicana de AI
Ap. Postal No. 20-217
San Angel
CP 01000 Mexico DF

Tel: +52 5 658 9402 Ext. 59
Telex: 1771632 VISAME (ATT
AMNISTIA INTERNACIONAL)

NEPAL
Please send *all* correspondence via the
IS, Campaign and Membership
Department

NETHERLANDS
Amnesty International
Dutch Section
Keizergracht 620
1017 ER Amsterdam

Tel: +31 20 26 44 36
Fax: +31 20 24 08 89
Telex: 18374 AINL

NEW ZEALAND
Amnesty International
New Zealand Section
P.O. Box 664, Te Aro
Wellington 1

Tel: +64 4 849 774
Fax: +64 4 845 949
Telex: 3561 METAL IMP ATT
AMNESTY
(for limited use only)

NIGERIA
Amnesty International
Nigerian Section
P.M.B. 59 Agodi
Ibadan
Oyo State

NORWAY
Amnesty International
Norwegian Section
Maridalsveien 87
0461 Oslo 4

Tel: +47 2 38 00 32
Fax: +47 2 37 53 86
Telex: 78898 AINAN

PERU
Señores
Casilla 581
Lima 18

Tel: +51 14 466 772
Fax: +51 14 713 700
Telex: 25202PE tel. 466772
PBHCSAR

PORTUGAL
Seccão Portugesa AI
Apartado 1642
1016 Lisboa Codex

Tel: +351 1 523 537
Telex: 64321 AMNST P

PUERTO RICO
Calle Cabo Alverio 562
Ext. Roosevelt Hato Rey
San Juan 00918

Tel: +1 809 767 7095

SENEGAL
Amnesty International
Section Senegalaise
126 rue Joseph Gomis (ex rue de
Bayeux)
B.P. 3813, Dakar

Tel: +221 22 10 86
Telex: 21754 SENLAW. SG
att. Bacre Waly Ndiaye
Cable: SENAMNY

SPAIN
Amnesty International
Paseo de Recoletos 18, Piso 6
28001 Madrid

Tel: +34 1 276 4118
Telex: 47344 AIES E

SWEDEN
Amnesty International
Swedish Section
Gyllenstiernsgatan 18
S-115 26 Stockholm

Tel: +46 8 663 1900
Fax: +46 8 662 7322
Telex: 12258 Amnesty S

SWITZERLAND
Amnesty International
Swiss Section
P.O. Box 1051
CH − 3001 Bern

Tel: +41 31 25 79 66
Telex: 911906 AMNS CH

TANZANIA
AI Tanzanian Section
National Secratariat
P.O. Box 4904
Dar es Salaam

Tel: +255 51 63008

TRINIDAD AND TOBAGO
Amnesty International
Trinidad and Tobago Section
P.O. Bag 231 Woodbrook P.O.
Port of Spain, TRINIDAD
West Indies

Tel: +1 809 627 6050

TUNISIA
AI Tunisian Section
BP 256
1002 Belvédère

TURKEY
Please send *all* correspondence via the
IS, Campaign and Membership
Department

UNITED KINGDOM
Amnesty International
5 Roberts Place
off Bowling Green Lane
London
EC1 0EJ

Tel: +44 1 251 8371
Fax: +44 1 251 1558
Telex: 917621 AIBS G
ATT BRITISH SECTION

USA
Amnesty International of the USA
(AIUSA)
322 8th Ave,
New York, NY 10001

Tel: +1 212 807 8400
Fax: +1 212 463 9193
Telex: 666628 AMNESTY

**AIUSA (WASHINGTON
OFFICE)**
Amnesty International
608 Massachusetts Avenue, NE
Washington DC 20002
USA

Tel: +1 202 544 0200
Fax: + 1 202 546 7142
Telex: 8229592

VENEZUELA
Señores Amnistia Internacional
Apartado 5110
Caracas 1010

Tel: +58 2 575 3279

These sections are serviced by the
International Secretariat (IS),
located at:
Amnesty International
International Secretariat
1 Easton Street
London WC1X 8DJ
UNITED KINGDOM

Tel: +44 1 833 1771
Fax: +44 1 833 5100
Telex: 28502

ACKNOWLEDGMENTS

Because of the extreme time pressure under which this book was produced, it would never have been possible without the help, understanding and co-operation of dozens of people. In particular, my wife, Eliza Wing, provided much-needed support and enthusiasm, not only during the actual tour but also in the many months leading up to it. In addition she also contributed her own writing and reporting skills and is responsible for the profiles of the five human-rights activists. My gratitude and love go first and foremost to her.

A huge thank-you, and lots of love, must also go to Jack Healey and Mary Daly, who enlisted me for this project, kept my spirits up when things seemed bleak, and made sure that everyone involved in the tour both co-operated and understood the importance of this book. In addition, Jessica Neuwirth and Glen Metsch-Ampel proved invaluable allies, opening many doors, solving numerous problems and providing information and, at times, comfort. Jamie Radner, Kelly Rappuchi, Richard Reoch, Franca Sciuto, Bill Pace, Claude Isakov and almost everyone at both Amnesty International and the Concerts for Human Rights Foundation who also helped turn this book into reality.

Jon Landau spent many hours with me, sharing his insights and his knowledge of both the tour and the music business. I am extremely grateful to him and to the other managers and their associates: Barbara Carr, Miles Copeland, Kim Turner, Billy Francis, Gail Colson, Elliot Roberts, Frank Gironda, Ron Perfit and Verna Gillis. In addition, George Travis, Bill Graham, Chris Chappell, Steven DePaul, Shelly Lazar, Tricia Aleck, Bob Koch, Larry Ahern and Tim Bernett all helped make the journey a little less bumpy for me. Thanks also to everyone at Reebok, especially Angel Martinez.

At *Rolling Stone* magazine, Jann S. Wenner, Robert Wallace and Susan Murcko not only supported me during this project, but, over the past twelve years, have provided me with a constant source of friendship and inspiration. In addition, special thanks to Cathy Mayer, the best assistant anyone could ask for. My agent, Michael Carlisle, has had an undue amount of patience with me over the years, and I thank him for his help. Thanks also to Reid Bostes and David Grossman, the agents for Amnesty International.

At Bloomsbury, David Reynolds had the courage to undertake a project that involved an unreasonable amount of effort and commitment. Special thanks also go to his assistant, Penny Phillips; to the project's editor, Helen Armitage; to the designers, Laurence Bradbury and Roy Williams. Thanks also to the production team: Sid Blakeborough, Chris Myers and the staff at Bookworm Typesetting; Robin Tang and Universal Colour Scanning; and to Roger Hawkins, Andreas Bonilla and everyone at Graficas in London, and Printer in Barcelona. And, of course, extra special thanks to the photographers, Neal Preston, Annie Leibovitz and Ken Regan; to the photo assistant, Paul Schiraldi; and to Kim Ronis, the photo editor and over-all assistant. I must also mention Betty Wing, whose translating skills came in handy early on in the project and who, along with Nat Wing, has shared her love with me over the years. Thanks.

Finally, a huge debt is owed to the artists— Bruce Springsteen, Peter Gabriel, Sting, Tracy Chapman and Youssou N'Dour—and their bands. Without them, none of this would have ever happened.

James Henke
Croton-on-Hudson, New York
October 1988

Stop press:

Good news - since Sting wrote his introduction (page 9), Sita Ram Maskey has been released from goal by the Nepalese government.